Walking With God Devotional

"Your 60 day journey to intimacy"

Ademola Ogunyanwo

Copyright © 2015 by Ademola Ogunyanwo

ISBN – 978-1523288571

Printed in the United Kingdom

Published by CreateSpace

Acknowledgments

I would like to first of all thank my Heavenly Father, my Lord Jesus Christ and the Holy Spirit for giving me the wisdom and inspiration to write this book.

I would like to thank my mother and father for bringing me up in a godly way and for giving me wise counsel. Mum and Dad, you have been very helpful to me. God bless you for all your selfless efforts towards seeing my success. Thank you for your love and prayers. I love you with my whole heart.

Special thanks to my Pastor Adedayo Babalola. Thank you for your patience and support in helping me with this book. Thank you for your love and prayers. You are indeed a role model, great man of God, and great inspiration to me. I really thank God for bringing you into my life, it is an honour. I love you with my whole heart.

Minister Ruky Obahor, my mother in the faith. Thank you so much. Your life and ministry is a living testimony. Thank you for all your selfless effort in making sure I am well equipped. Thank you for your love and prayers. Thank you for having me as a son, it is a privilege. I just want to say, thank you and God bless you richly.

A huge thank you to all my friends who have aided me over the years in my spiritual growth, I wouldn't have made it without you. Eseoghene Okhuakhua, Stella King, Vandross Farinto, Andrew Harris, Kalada Osunpuju, Emmanual Williams, James Onyekwere, Esther Grey, Christian Olu Israel, Benjamin Ajala, Esther Berry, Wonu Olumoroti and many more. You have all been a blessing to me and I love you all.

Finally, thank you so much Pastor Tunji Ogunjimi. You are indeed sent from God. Without you and without God, this book will only remain a day dream. God richly bless you.

Contents

vii

The Spirit of Sonship

1 John 3:1

"Behold, what manner of love the Father hath bestowed upon us, that we should be called the sons of God."(KJV)

The word "Behold" means consider, observe, or take a look at. If I were to rephrase this verse, it would sound like this: "Look at, consider, or observe the manner or the kind of love the Father has for us, that we should be called His sons/daughters."

When Adam committed treason against God in the Garden of Eden, what Adam lost wasn't really just the blessing; that was a part of it, but what Adam lost was his position as a Son of God. How do I know this? Luke 3:38 declares that Adam was the son of God. God lost a relationship with His son Adam, and because of Adam's sin, death spread to everyone. This automatically meant that God lost a relationship with the entire human race. God created man to fellowship with, and that was what He lost when Adam fell. For this reason, God sent Jesus to bring us back to our position of sonship. Hebrews 2:9-11 says, **"Yes, by God's grace, Jesus tasted death for everyone. God, for whom and through whom everything was made, chose to bring many children (sons) into glory. And it was only right that He should make Jesus, through His suffering, a perfect leader, fit to bring them into their salvation. So now Jesus and the ones He makes holy have the same**

Father. That is why Jesus is not ashamed to call them His brothers and sisters." (He is talking about us.)

Jesus is your blood brother and by the reason of His death and the power of the Holy Spirit, you now have access to God the Father (see Ephesians 2:18). You and Jesus have the same Father. This means that God loves you in the same way He loves Jesus (John 17:23). According to God's word in Galatians 4:7, which says, **"Wherefore thou art no more a servant, but a son; and if a son, then an heir of God through Christ."** You are a son. You have the exact same privileges as Christ. I didn't say it; the word of God says it. The word of God tells us in Romans 5:2, **"Because of our faith, Christ has brought us into this place of undeserved privilege where we now stand."** Where is this place of underserved privilege where we now stand? Our place of sonship. Jesus bought us back to our position as sons and daughters of God! Hallelujah. The word of God tells us in John 1:12:13, **"But as many as received Him, to them gave He power to become the sons of God, even to them that believe on His name: Which were born, not of blood, nor of the will of the flesh, nor of the will of man, but of God."**

Let this truth sink into your spirit. Redemption gave you and I the power to become sons of God in Christ.

God loves you and I so much that He gave us this privilege to be called sons of God. We didn't do anything to earn it; it was given to us as a gift. All we did was accept it the moment we gave our lives to Christ. When we give our lives to Christ, God sends the Spirit of His Son into our hearts, prompting us to call out, "Abba, Father!" (Galatians 4:6) Praise God for this awesome privilege. As a son of God, you have authority to rule and reign just as God the Father, Son and Holy Spirit rules and reigns.

2

The Good News of Jesus Christ

Romans 1:16

"For I am not ashamed of this good news about Christ. It is the power of God at work, saving everyone who believes—the Jew first and also the Gentile For in it is the righteousness of God revealed from faith to faith: as it is written, 'The just shall live by faith.'"(NLT version)

The book of Romans is a very interesting book. I got so excited reading chapter one. I was in awe of Paul's explanation of how much God loves us. The book reveals to us so much about the righteousness that God has given us. Get excited with me as we go through a little journey about a verse in Romans chapter 1.

The first question I asked myself was what is this good news of Jesus Christ? Jesus has done so much but here is one:

- 1 Timothy 1:15, **"This is a trustworthy saying, and everyone should accept it: 'Christ Jesus came into the world to save sinners'—and I am the worst of them all.'"**

When the Bible says, "This is a trustworthy saying," it means: this is real. Jesus came to die for the entire world. We were all sinners, dead in our sins, hell bound, and doomed for eternal punishment. We were enemies of God and deserved death, but the book of Ephesians 2:4-6, 8 tells us: **"But God, being rich in mercy, because of His great love with which He loved us, even when we were dead** in our transgressions, made us alive together with Christ (by grace you have been saved.) For by grace (The unmerited favours of God through Jesus Christ) you have been saved through faith; and that not of yourselves, it is the gift of God." Your salvation is a gift from God. You didn't earn it, but God initiated it (I call Him the God of initiative) and gave it to you. All you did was receive it by faith when you heard the good news about Christ. This is the good news that saved you.

The first part of Ephesians 2 gives us a picture of what our lives were like before we came to Christ. We were doomed for punishment, but I love how God interrupted Satan with His love. As the Bible says, "But God who is rich in mercy..." This gives us an insight into who God is. "Merciful." This is what sinners and even Christians need to hear. That God is merciful. Many times, we tell people about judgment, but not love and mercy. People know so much about the judgement of God and that they will go hell, but little is spoken about mercy. Though I believe in judgment, I believe much more in mercy.

Let me round off with this so that I can give you a clearer picture of what the apostle Paul is saying in Ephesians 2:4-6. The word *grace* in Hebrew is "CHEN" from a root word "CHANAN", which means to bend or stoop in kindness to another as a superior to an inferior. The word *mercy* in Hebrew is "hesed", meaning God's covenant loving-kindness. The apostle Paul is saying that God, because of His loving-kindness towards us, stooped so low in kindness to reach out to a fallen, wretched and doomed world through Jesus Christ and gave us a life we didn't deserve through the death of His son. Isn't that beautiful that a sinner who is doomed in drugs, sex, alcohol, the occult, and all sorts can actually be saved? I mean, that is the highest act of mercy and love. This is the good news of Jesus Christ that Paul is talking about in Romans 1:16. This is what we ought to tell sinners: they can be saved. There is so much more to share with you, but I do hope this has blessed you greatly.

Remain ever blessed.

You Have the Same Father as Jesus

Hebrews 2:11

"So now Jesus and the ones He makes Holy have the same Father." (NLT)

I don't know about you but it's good news to me that Jesus and I have the same Father. Think of this for a minute. This means that in the same way that Jesus has access to the Father, as a born again child of God, you can rest assured that you also have access to God the Father's presence.

In Isaiah 59:2, the Bible says, "**But your iniquities have made a separation between you and your God, and your sins have hidden His face from you so that He does not hear.**" It is important that we put this scripture into perspective. This was the old covenant and the people were judged based on what they did. Under the new covenant, Christ has been judged on our behalf. Today, the blood of Jesus that was shed for mankind appeases God. The sin issue has been settled and we have been made holy through our Lord Jesus. The Bible says in Ephesians 2:14, "**For Christ Himself has brought peace to us. He united Jews and Gentiles into one people when, in His own body on the cross, He broke down the wall of hostility that separated us.**" Jesus brought peace to us by dying for us on the cross of Calvary. The grace of our Lord Jesus provided a way for a sinful person to be forgiven and cleansed from his unrighteousness. A believer is the "forgiven one". The truth is that God has already in Christ paid the price for the sins of the world, but the believer is one who receives what God has done. Everything God does must be received.

6

Under the old covenant, people approached God with guilt, shame, fear, and timidity. They were afraid of God and the curse that would fall upon them when they sinned. Jesus came to break that bondage. Under the new covenant, you do not have to fear. You can come to God boldly because Jesus has fully paid the price for your sin nature and now you have a righteous nature that is just like that of God.

What's my point? Once you accept Jesus Christ as Lord and Saviour of your life, you now have the same Father as Jesus. This means you have the same privileges as Jesus does. You can now have access to the Father just like Jesus. Ephesians 2:18 says, **"Now all of us can come to the Father through the same Holy Spirit because of what Christ has done for us. So now, you Gentiles are no longer strangers and foreigners. You are citizens along with all of God's holy people. You are members of God's family."** Did you read that? You are a member of God's family! This means that, because of Jesus Christ, you are entitled to everything God has. Through Jesus, God becomes your Father. Galatians 4:6-7 says, **"Because you are sons, God has sent forth the Spirit of His Son into our hearts, crying, 'Abba! Father!' Therefore you are no longer a slave, but a son; and if a son, then an heir through God."** Praise God.

God's love for you is revealed in Christ. God loves you the same way He loves Jesus. I didn't say it, Jesus prayed it, and we can see this in the book of John 17:22-23, **"The glory which You have given Me I have given to them, that they may be one, just as We are one; I in them and You in Me, that they may be perfected in unity, so that the world may know that You sent Me, and loved them, even as You have loved Me."** If you want to know how much God loves you, then look at Christ, and study His life. Jesus was never once sick; He never lacked food or money. He operated in all the gifts of God. He was filled with love, performed miracles etc. God wants the same for you. How do I know this? Romans 8:39 says, "**...nothing in all creation will ever be able to separate us from the love of God that is revealed in Christ Jesus our Lord.**"

The Power of Joy, Faith and Patience

James 1:3-5

"Dear brothers and sisters, when troubles of any kind come your way, consider it an opportunity for great joy. For you know that when your faith is tested, your endurance has a chance to grow. So let it grow, for when your endurance is fully developed, you will be perfect and complete, needing nothing. If you need wisdom, ask our generous God, and He will give it to you. He will not rebuke you for asking. But when you ask Him, be sure that your faith is in God alone. Do not waver, for a person with divided loyalty is as unsettled as a wave of the sea that is blown and tossed by the wind. Such people should not expect to receive anything from the Lord. Their loyalty is divided between God and the world, and they are unstable in everything they do."

Are you weary and almost feel like giving up? Do you find yourself almost wanting to say, "I quit"? There are times I feel like saying the same thing, but as they say, "Winners do not quit and quitters do not win." You and I are winners and God has given us all it takes for us to win. In this piece, I will be showing you certain things that are needed to live that victorious life God has called us to live. I pray that as you read this, you are blessed and strengthened to carry on in Jesus' name.

The Bible says that we should consider it an opportunity for great joy when trials come our way. Oh, come on! Let's be real with ourselves! The last thing you and I want to do is to be joyful when we encounter trials. It's like telling someone

9

to cheer up when they have just lost their job and are deep in debt. However, the scripture highlights that the trials we face actually give us the opportunity to be joyful. Before I go any further, let me first let you know that the reason we face trials is because of the word of God. Jesus, explaining in the parable of the sower in Mark 4:17 said, "Persecution comes for the word's sake." This simply means that when you receive God's word concerning any area of your life, Satan will come to challenge that word. God said concerning Jesus in Matthew 3:17 **"This is my beloved son in whom I am well pleased"** and after Jesus fasted for 40 days and was hungry, the devil tempted Him (Matthew 4:4). Satan challenged Him in the area of His identity because God said, "This is my Beloved Son" but because Jesus was rooted in God's word, He defeated Satan with God's word.

Now, we have established that the reason that believers encounter trials is because of God's word. When trials come our way as believers, we should remain joyful. Jesus told His disciples in the book of Matthew 5:11-12, **"Blessed are you when people insult you and persecute you, and falsely say all kinds of evil against you because of Me. Rejoice and be glad, for your reward in heaven is great; for in the same way they persecuted the prophets who were before you."**

The next verse in James chapter 1:3 tells us that our faith is tested in the midst of trials. Everybody goes through trials. Once you have received the word of God and have joy, be prepared because that word will be tested. Do you remember that Jesus also said in Mark 4:17 that some who receive God's word with joy will wither when persecution arises because they have no root? What is the root? Faith in the word of God. May I add, trials do not grow your faith, but trials test your faith. Your faith is rooted and grown from God's word (Romans 10:17). When persecution arises,

10

remain joyful and remain in the word of God. Read God's word over and over again till it's rooted in you. As you remain joyful, meditating on God's promises, the fruit it produces in you is the force of patience. Patience is not being passive; patience is the art of waiting on God in prayer, fasting, word study and carrying out other instructions from His word whilst waiting for the promise to come to pass. As a matter of fact, the promise comes to pass whilst carrying out the instructions God gives us in His word. You want to be financially blessed? Give your tithes, offerings and any other things God asks you to give whilst waiting on God to enlarge your financial status. That is what we call patience. The word tells us to allow patience to grow. The means allow the word of God to grow the patience in you. Once you allow patience to grow, the Bible promises that you will be perfect. Yes, perfect and needing nothing.

True Worship

John 4:24

"God is a Spirit: and they that worship Him must worship Him in spirit and in truth."

I meditated on this and asked a question: what does it mean to worship in truth and in spirit? Man is a threefold being and we see this in 1 Thessalonians 5:23, **"May your whole spirit, soul and body be kept blameless at the coming of our Lord Jesus Christ."** The spirit part of a person is the part that God uses to communicate with a person. The Bible tells us in the above scripture that true worship is born out of a person's spirit. This is made possible by the Holy Spirit, as Jesus said in John 7:38, **"He who believes in Me, as the Scripture said, 'From his innermost being (spirit being) will flow rivers of living water. By this He spoke of the Spirit."** Worship is not just limited to singing songs. A heart that is filled with a revelation of what Christ has done can indeed worship in spirit and in truth. When worship springs from a heart acquainted with what God has done for us in Christ and magnifies God for this, this is called new covenant worship.

Let me explain further. Deuteronomy 6:4 says, **"Love the LORD your God with all your heart and with all your soul and with all your strength."** This was the demand of the old covenant, and in fact, no one could actually do this in truth. However, under the new covenant, God has saved us, washed us, forgiven us, accepted us, made us His sons, made us righteous, given us His Spirit, loved us and blessed us.

12

God did the loving and what happens is that as we start to comprehend all that God has done for us, we start to respond to His love and this leads us to worship. Worship is the response of a heart that knows what God as done for him/ her through the death and resurrection of Jesus Christ. Worship under the new covenant stems from about 4 basic truths: Under the new covenant we worship God based on what Christ *has done* for us, and what Christ *is doing* for us (presently our High Priest at the right hand of the Father making intercession for us). It also stems from what the word has said about us and what the word is saying about us. The scriptures say that we love Him because He loved us first. Therefore, worship is a fruit of Christianity and not the root.

Loving the Lord Jesus Christ comes from your heart and then reflects on your mind and actions. Mere actions are just legalism and religion.

To worship in spirit and truth therefore simply means to reverence our Lord based on what He did for us through Jesus Christ.

His Love is Constant

Lamentations 3: 22

"The steadfast love of the Lord never ceases; His mercies never come to an end; they are new every morning; great is your faithfulness."

The word of God says what it means and means exactly what it says. God's love for us is constant, and it never changes. Maybe you have messed up in the past and you feel condemned, but God still loves you and is willing to forgive you. How am I sure about this? Ephesians 1:7 tells us, "**In Him we have redemption through His blood, the forgiveness of sins, in accordance with the riches of God's grace,**" and 1 John 1:9 tells us, "**If we confess our sins, He is faithful and just to forgive us our sins, and to cleanse us from all unrighteousness.**" His love for you will get rid of the sin in your life. When you get a revelation of God's love for you, sin will loosen its grip over your life. His love will transform you into a new person, praise God!

God is good and His mercy endures forever (Psalm 136:1). God's mercies never run out; you can rest assured you have His mercy every morning. When you wake in the morning, receive God's mercy for that day. Appreciate the Lord for His mercy upon your life. The same scripture says, "Great is thy faithfulness." This means that God is determined to be faithfully merciful to you. We do not deserve His mercy, yet He chose to be merciful to you and me. David said, "**For His anger lasts only a moment, but His favour lasts a lifetime! Weeping may last through the night, but joy comes with the morning.**" (Psalm 30:5). God's favour is for a lifetime. This means that you can receive favour anytime, any day, anywhere and if there be any areas in your life that you need to repent of, do so and receive God's mercy that lasts for a lifetime. I love the truth of God's word that says, "Joy comes with the morning." This means that every time we wake up, one of the benefits of that day is joy. Receive joy each day because the joy of the Lord is your strength for that day (Nehemiah 8:10).

I love the song that says, "Great is thy faithfulness x2, morning by morning new mercies I see. All I have needed thy hand has provided. Great is thy faithfulness Lord unto me!"

Receive God's love, mercy and faithfulness today. You are blessed in Jesus' precious Name.

Remember, God's love is constant; it never changes.

Inseparable Love

Romans 8:35-39

"Who shall separate us from the love of Christ? *Shall* tribulation, or distress, or persecution, or famine, or nakedness, or peril, or sword? As it is written: 'For Your sake we are killed all day long; we are accounted as sheep for the slaughter.' Yet in all these things we are more than conquerors through Him who loved us. For I am persuaded that neither death nor life, nor angels nor principalities nor powers, nor things present nor things to come, nor height nor depth, nor any other created thing, shall be able to separate us from the love of God which is in Christ Jesus our Lord."

I love how Paul starts this passage of scripture with a question, "Who shall separate us from the love of Christ?" I personally believe that the reason Paul asked "who" is because people will tell you or have already told you that God doesn't love you. Or people may have mistreated you, and as a result you feel unloved. The truth is that no matter what people say or do, they cannot change God's mind, He will keep on loving you. God loves you even if you are at fault. God loves you so much that even if your parents abandon you, or mistreat you, He will take care of you. King David said in his Psalm, Psalm 27:10, **"Though my father and mother forsake me, the LORD will receive me."** The Lord will receive you and love you irrespective of your circumstances.

God loves you irrespective of the hardship going on in the world. God's love for you will keep you secure regardless of the happenings around you. His word says in 1 John 4:18 (NIV), **"There is no fear in love. But perfect love drives out fear, because fear has to do with punishment. The one who fears is not made perfect in love."** Once you understand how much your Heavenly Father loves you, you won't need to fear. King David understood this love so that he could boldly say in Psalm 23:4 (NIV), **"Yea, though I walk through the valley of the shadow of death, I will fear no evil: for thou art with me; thy rod and thy staff they comfort me."** He could also write in Psalm 24:1-3: "The LORD is my light and my salvation— whom shall I fear? The LORD is the stronghold of my life— of whom shall I be afraid? When the wicked advance against me to devour me, it is my enemies and my foes who will stumble and fall. Though an army besiege me, my heart will not fear; though war break out against me, even then I will be confident." King David's confidence was rooted in God's Love for him.

Verse 37 of Romans 8 says, **"In all these things, we are more than conquerors through Him who loved us."** This means that as a believer, you have the power to overcome anything through the love of Christ. Knowing that Christ loves you should give you the confidence to overcome anything you are currently going through. Through Christ's love, you are the victor and not the victim. The scripture goes on to say in verses 38 and 39, **"For I am persuaded that neither death nor life, nor angels nor principalities nor powers, nor things present nor things to come, nor height nor depth, nor any other created thing, shall be able to separate us from the love of God which is in Christ Jesus our Lord."** As a believer, you have got to be fully persuaded, convinced, and assured that there is no demonic force that can separate you from God's love. Settle

17

it in your heart that God loves you regardless of what comes your way. Satan cannot receive love, and therefore he will try to deceive you and make you feel that your shortcomings and circumstances will distance God's love for you. That is a lie. Paul told the church in Ephesus: **"Then Christ will make His home in your hearts as you trust in Him. Your roots will grow down into God's love and keep you strong. And may you have the power to understand, as all God's people should, how wide, how long, how high, and how deep His love is. May you experience the love of Christ, though it is too great to understand fully. Then you will be made complete with all the fullness of life and power that comes from God."** The reason for such a prayer is that anyone who is rooted, rested, and abiding in God's love will be the most confident person on earth. Once you are persuaded that God loves you no matter what, Satan will not be able to shift you and your faith in God's word will stand strong. Praise God!

Abide in His Love and His word for the rest of your life and believe me, you will be the most confident person on earth.

Righteousness, The Key to Answered Prayer

J ames 5:16

"The earnest prayer of a righteous person has great power and produces wonderful results."

The first question I want to ask is this: who is the righteous person? Pause and think about it for a moment. The righteous person is not the person who tries to live right based on their behaviour, nor is the righteous person someone who is nice in their own eyes. According to Galatians 2:16, the Bible says, "**Yet we know that a person is made right with God by faith in Jesus Christ, not by obeying the law. And we have believed in Christ Jesus, so that we might be made right with God because of our faith in Christ, not because we have obeyed the law. For no one will ever be made right with God by obeying the law.**" The scripture is simply saying that we are not made right with God based on what we do; we are made right with God based on faith in Jesus Christ. As a result of our faith in Jesus, we become righteous. Therefore, our faith in Him will produce the type of right living that comes from God and pleases God. In other words, the righteous person is one who is made right with God through faith in Jesus Christ only.

The opening scripture says that because you are a righteous person, your prayers have power and produce wonderful results. This means you can expect your prayers to be answered all the time because you are the righteousness of

19

God in Christ. When you pray, pray based on your right-standing with God. Declare your righteousness and expect to see answers to what you ask for, as long as they are His will. I hope this stirs up your faith, because you are God's righteousness. Never forget that your prayers produce wonderful results. As sons of God, you can expect to be healed, or delivered from anxiety. You can expect your son/daughter and spouse to be restored to you, expect your children to be saved, expect progression in your career, and expect to overcome addictions because you are the righteousness of God in Christ Jesus. Express that you are the righteousness of God through daily confession. Settle it in your heart that you are righteous because the Bible says in Romans 10:10, **"For it is by believing in your heart that you are made right with God, and it is by confessing with your mouth that you are saved."** The word "saved" means delivered. Once you settle it in your heart that you are righteous, confess your desire with your mouth. It is not good enough to just believe, but you must also confess and act on God's word.

This, my brethren, is the best way to see your prayers answered. Your prayers are answered based on your faith in Jesus and the truth that Jesus made you right with God, praise God. Expect your prayers to be answered because you are the righteousness of God in Christ Jesus.

How to Live Triumphantly Over Sin

Romans 5:17

"For the sin of this one man, Adam, caused death to rule over many. But even greater is God's wonderful grace and His gift of righteousness, for all who receive it will live in triumph over sin and death through this one man, Jesus Christ."

Are you struggling with sin in your life? If so, you do not have to struggle anymore because the word of God has the answer to your problem. First, I want you to understand that sin has already been dealt with at the cross of Calvary. Romans 6:5-11 says, **"For if we have been united with Him in a death like His, we will certainly also be united with Him in a resurrection like His. For we know that our old self was crucified with Him so that the body ruled by sin might be done away with, that we should no longer be slaves to sin— because anyone who has died has been set free from sin. Now if we died with Christ, we believe that we will also live with Him. For we know that since Christ was raised from the dead, He cannot die again; death no longer has mastery over Him. The death He died, He died to sin once for all; but the life He lives, He lives to God. In the same way, count yourselves dead to sin but alive to God in Christ Jesus."** As a born again believer, the day you got baptised, you were baptised into the death of Jesus Christ, and just as sin and death have no power over Jesus, because you are in Him, sin has no power over you. The reason why many still struggle with sin is because they are ignorant of the fact that sin no longer has power over them. Romans 6:14 says, **"For sin shall no longer be your master, because you are not under the law, but under grace."** The word grace here means unmerited favour, and divine empowerment. Through the grace that has been given to us, sin has no power over you.

I ask the question again, if all this has been done for us, why are some people still struggling with sin? To explain, if I called you and told you that I had put a million pounds into your account, the money wouldn't do you any good if you did not make use of it. The grace and the gift of righteousness of God work in the same way. Through Jesus Christ, sin has been dealt with, but as the opening scripture says, to live triumphantly over sin, you have to daily consciously *receive* the wonderful gift of grace and of righteousness. The word righteousness means right standing with God. God does not give you His righteousness based on your behaviour, whether good or bad, but He gives it to you as a gift through accepting Jesus as your Lord and Saviour. The day you accepted Christ, you were made right with God, you received His gift of grace and righteousness. You may slip up every now and then but in the same way that you put on your clothes every day, you must daily and consciously put on your gift of righteousness. Righteousness is a garment that you put on (Isaiah 61:10; Job 29:14 and Ephesians 6:14).

How do I put on my clothes of righteousness? Romans 10:10, **"For with the heart man believeth unto righteousness; and with the mouth confession is made unto salvation."** This scripture is saying that you must believe that you are righteous. At all times, believe you are righteous even when you don't feel like it. As a born again child of God in Christ, you are righteous. The more you believe you are righteous, the more you will want to act right. It is not enough to only believe, but you must confess that you are righteous. Confess, "Jesus Christ has made me righteous." Say it every day whether you feel righteous or not. For instance, you might be struggling with foul language, pornography, smoking etc. Keep believing and confessing that you are the righteousness of God, and that sin has no power over you because you are under grace. The more you keep saying this, sooner or later, you will stop doing those things. This is what the Bible means when it says that you will live triumphantly over sin and death. The more you believe and confess, the less you will want to sin. Notice that sin leads to death. Therefore, fight it with the confession of, 'I am the righteousness of God." When you go to God in prayer, say, "Lord, I believe that You made me righteous through the death of Jesus, therefore I receive my gift of grace and righteousness to overcome sin. I confess my fault to you Lord and I declare that because I am your righteousness, this sin no longer has power over me. I receive my forgiveness given to me through Jesus Christ and I turn away from this sin. In Jesus' name, amen.

In Jesus Christ and Through Jesus Christ

Romans 10: 17

"So faith comes from hearing, that is, hearing the Good News about Christ."

Nowadays, we hear so much about faith. We know that we need faith to please God as the Bible says in Hebrews 11:6, **"Without faith it is impossible to please God."** So we are going to go back to some important fundamentals about faith. The first question to ask then is: what is faith? Hebrews 11:1 tells us, **"Faith is the confidence that what we hope for will actually happen; it gives us assurance about things we cannot see."** Faith gives you confidence that everything you believe and expect from God's word will happen though you have not seen it manifest physically. That is Bible faith. Now then, to stir up this faith, Romans 10:17 tells us that this faith comes by hearing the good news of Jesus Christ. The Bible is not just a book; it is a book about the goodness of Jesus Christ from Genesis all the way to Revelation. This means that Jesus should be the central focus of your faith and everything we believe and do should result from our faith in Jesus' finished work.

So then, what is this good news about Jesus Christ? Before I answer this question, let me mention that Jesus is the way to victory in every area of your life. As a matter of fact, as a born again Christian, Jesus *is* your life and without Jesus, you are nothing.

The book of Romans in chapters 5 and 6 tells us the Good News we have in Jesus and through Jesus. Praise God.

Romans 5:15: **"But there is a great difference between Adam's sin and God's gracious gift. For the sin of this one man, Adam, brought death to many. But even greater is God's wonderful grace and His gift of forgiveness to many through this other man, Jesus Christ"** (NLT). Praise God that through Jesus Christ, God's wonderful grace and gift of forgiveness abounds towards us. Ephesians 1:7 tells us, **"In Him we have redemption and through His blood the forgiveness of sins."** This is good news, because without Jesus, we are all doomed for eternal punishment, but through Jesus and in Jesus we have the forgiveness of sin. This certainly does not mean we should live life carelessly. NO! It does mean that when we make mistakes, we can get rid of whatever it is that was holding us back by running to Jesus.

Romans 5:17, **"For the sin of this one man, Adam, caused death to rule over many. But even greater is God's wonderful grace and His gift of righteousness, for all who receive it will live in triumph over sin and death through this one man, Jesus Christ."** (NLT) The scripture doesn't say we will stop sinning and live righteously if we try to. No, the scripture tells us that if we receive God's free grace and gift of righteousness, we will live triumphantly over sin and death through Jesus Christ. Through Jesus, you and I have the ability to live triumphantly over any sinful habits, whether small or big, praise God. Many people teach that to be accepted by God, you have to behave well and live rightly NO, NO, NO! God accepting us results in our living right through Jesus Christ. The reason why you and I desire to live right is because we understand that God has accepted us.

Romans 5:21 says, **"So that, just as sin reigned in death, so also grace will reign through righteousness, resulting**

in eternal life through Jesus Christ our Lord." (Holman Bible)

Right now, in this day and age, grace reigns because of our Lord Jesus Christ. We live in the era of God's bountiful grace, and we live in the era of enjoying the love and goodness of God that comes through Jesus Christ. Because we live under the grace of God, sin does not have dominion over us. God's grace is the antidote for sin. Through Jesus, grace reigns.

Romans 6:10-11 says, **"For the death that He died, He died to sin once for all; but the life that He lives, He lives to God. Even so consider yourselves to be dead to sin, but alive to God in Christ Jesus."**

Through Jesus and in Jesus, you and I are dead to the power of sin and alive to God. All thanks and praise to God through Jesus for all Jesus has done.

The Greatest Act of Love

2 Corinthians 9:7-9

"For God loves a person who gives cheerfully."

God is love and there is no argument about that. The truth is that God loves everybody whether a sinner or a believer, but God deals with everyone differently. God has no favourites, but there are certain things that some people do that touch God's heart and cause Him to react in a way that it looks like He loves some people more than He loves others. The Bible clearly gives two categories of people that touch the heart of God: a soul winner (Proverbs 11:30) and a cheerful giver (2 Corinthians 9:7-9). Today, I would like to talk about a cheerful giver.

Though I have read this scripture time after time, for strange reasons, my eyes suddenly opened as I studied it again today. The Amplified version of this scripture say, **"For God loves (He takes pleasure in, prizes above other things, and is unwilling to abandon or to do without) a cheerful (joyous, 'prompt to do it') giver [whose heart is in his giving]."** I love the last part that says "whose heart is in his/her giving." Giving is not what you give; giving is an attitude. Giving is an act of love. When you give to your wife, children, friends and co-workers, you are simply expressing your love to them. Giving is the only way God expresses His love to us. The Bible says in John 3:16, **"God so loved the world that He gave His only begotten Son."** Giving is an expression of love. If you as a husband love your wife, you will give to her and vice-versa. Giving is an act of love. A cheerful giver whose heart is in his giving takes on the

27

nature of God. When you give in love, with joy, and promptly when God leads you, you put yourself in the position to receive.

Isn't it amazing that the scripture says that God is unwilling to abandon or do without a cheerful giver? This means that someone who gives is useful to God. What Paul is clearly saying is that God needs such individuals. I have been told many times that God can do without me, but now I realise that if I am a giver; He needs me and will do anything to keep me alive. This is not pride; I am only stating what the Bible says. I have noticed that giving is one of the simplest ways to grow in the things of God. The next verse says, **"And God is able to make all grace (every favour and earthly blessing) come to you in abundance."** This means that the more I give the more grace I get. I do not know about you, but I need more grace in my life.

If you are struggling to give, it's because you have forgotten that God gave and continually gives to you. Give in love and give in faith expecting to receive something from God. God gave His Son expecting a harvest of souls and you are one of them, so when you give, expect a harvest from God not men. Also remember, the greatest act of love is to give to someone who cannot pay you back.

So today, begin to look for ways to bless people starting with your fellow believers.

Now is The Time of God's Favour

2 Corinthians 6:2

"I tell you, now is the time of God's favour"(NIV)

Good, good news! The good news is that you have God's favour available to you now. Favour simply means grace. Let me explain to you as best as I can how God made His favour available to us.

In Luke chapter 2, The Bible gives an account of the event of Jesus' birth. Let us read verses 1-13:

"In those days Caesar Augustus issued a decree that a census should be taken of the entire Roman world. (This was the first census that took place while Quirinius was governor of Syria.) And everyone went to their own town to register. So Joseph also went up from the town of Nazareth in Galilee to Judea, to Bethlehem the town of David, because he belonged to the house and line of David. He went there to register with Mary, who was pledged to be married to him and was expecting a child. While they were there, the time came for the baby to be born, and she gave birth to her firstborn, a son. She wrapped Him in cloths and placed Him in a manger, because there was no guest room available for them. And there were shepherds living out in the fields nearby, keeping watch over their flocks at night. An angel of the Lord appeared to them, and the glory of the Lord shone around them, and they were terrified. But the angel said to them, "Do not be afraid. I bring you good news that will cause great joy for all the

29

people. **Today in the town of David a Saviour has been born to you; He is the Messiah, the Lord. This will be a sign to you: You will find a baby wrapped in cloths and lying in a manger."** Suddenly a great company of the heavenly host appeared with the angel, praising God and saying, "Glory to God in the highest heaven, and on earth peace to those on whom His favour rests (Or goodwill towards men).

Did you see that? "Peace to those whom His favour rest." Who are those on whom His favour rests? The redeemed of the Lord. The Amplified Bible tells us in Ephesians 2:5, '**It is by grace (His favour and mercy which you did not deserve) that you are saved."** As a redeemed child of God, you have God's favour now.

One of the many things that Jesus came to preach is God's favour. This is Jesus speaking in Luke 4:18-19: **"THE SPIRIT OF THE LORD IS UPON ME, BECAUSE HE ANOINTED ME TO PREACH THE GOSPEL TO THE POOR. HE HAS SENT ME TO PROCLAIM RELEASE TO THE CAPTIVES, AND RECOVERY OF SIGHT TO THE BLIND, TO SET FREE THOSE WHO ARE OPPRESSED, TO PROCLAIM THE FAVOURABLE YEAR OF THE LORD."** The (Amplified version says, **"To proclaim the accepted and acceptable year of the Lord, the day when salvation and THE FREE FAVOURS of God PROFUSELY ABOUNDS.)"**

The word profuse means plenty, so in other words, God's free favour is plentiful. Psalm 30:5 tells us that "**His favour lasts a lifetime."** This means that as long as you live, God's free favour abounds towards you. This favour will make things work for you without sweat; people will just like you irrespective of your inadequacy. This doesn't mean you shouldn't develop yourself. However, note that self-development is not good enough because you still need that favour of God.

God's favour is free and it is yours if you are a born again child of God. So remember, *now* is the time for God's favour, not tomorrow, NOW. So receive favour today in the name of Jesus. God's favour has nothing to do with your performance, but this doesn't give us the license to live carelessly. God's favour amongst many other things, leads men to repentance. God's favour will help you break any bad addictions. That is the whole point of grace, to help you live a life free from sin. Though grace is free, do not use it as an opportunity to serve sin. Favour is yours today, so go to the throne of God in prayer and receive your favour right now.

Now is The Time

Hebrews 11:1

"Now faith is..."

I will start off by saying that it is good to believe God for the future, but the truth is that faith is not just a future force, but faith is a now force. I always hear people saying, "one day this and that will happen" but I hardly hear anyone talking about what will happen now. By faith, you can command things to happen now. For instance, if you study the healing ministry of Jesus Christ, you will discover that most of the people He encountered received their healing immediately. Let us look at some scriptures together.

In Genesis 1, we read that God said, "'Let there be light" and there was light. Light didn't come a day after God said it, light came immediately. Someone might say, "Well, that's God- He can do anything." That's true, but what is also true is that you have ability in God and can command things too. As a new creation in Christ Jesus, you have God's kind of faith. Genesis 1:28 tells us that God created man in His own image and likeness, and if you are in Christ Jesus, you can get the same order of results as God. Jesus said in Mark 11:22, **"Have faith in God"** but the Greek text reads, **"Have the God kind of Faith."** The God kind of faith has no respect for time, age, and gender. The God kind of faith puts you above circumstances. You can receive what you need now with the God kind of faith. Let us see this from the scriptures:

In Mark chapter 10:46, we are told of a blind man named Bartimaeus who was sitting by the roadside begging. Let's look at the rest of the story from verse 47-52:

"When he heard that it was Jesus of Nazareth, he began to shout, 'Jesus, Son of David, have mercy on me!' Many rebuked him and told him to be quiet, but he shouted all the more, 'Son of David, have mercy on me!'

Jesus stopped and said, 'Call him.'

So they called to the blind man, 'Cheer up! On your feet! He's calling you.' Throwing his cloak aside, he jumped to his feet and came to Jesus. 'What do you want me to do for you?' Jesus asked him.

The blind man said, 'Rabbi, I want to see.'

'Go,' said Jesus, 'your faith has healed you.' Immediately he received his sight and followed Jesus along the road." **(NIV)**

A lot of times, we are shouting, "Jesus please help me!" and Jesus is saying, "What do you want me to do for you now?" Jesus knew the man needed sight but He had to ask the man so that he could respond in faith. The Bible says that he immediately received his sight. Jesus did not say, "Go, and come back tomorrow." NO, the moment Jesus touched his eyes, he received his sight. What I am trying to portray? Faith is now.

For some of you reading this, your problem may not be healing, but whatever it is that you need, it is available now. Every day you wake, awake expecting something good to happen to you, and expect that the long-awaited answer to your prayer is received now.

Brethren, you have got to believe that you will see the goodness of God now. I love what the apostle Paul said in 2 Corinthians 6:2, **"I tell you, now is the time of God's favour."** Notice that Paul didn't say that God's time of favour is tomorrow. No, he said that the time of God's favour is NOW. This means you can receive favour now, healing now, or a new job now. Whatever you need is available now.

Undeserved Privilege

Romans 5:1-2

"Therefore, since we have been made right in God's sight by faith, we have peace with God because of what Jesus Christ our Lord has done for us.

Because of our faith, Christ has brought us into this place of undeserved privilege where we now stand."

The above scripture shows us two things regarding the good news of what Jesus Christ did for us. The first one is that by accepting Jesus Christ as your personal Lord and Saviour, you have peace with God. If you are not in Christ, you do not have peace with God. If you are in Christ by faith, then you have been made righteous in God's sight and have peace with Him.

The second is that through Jesus Christ, you have an undeserved privilege. This is good news. The word privilege means a special right or an advantage. This means that if you are in Christ, you have an advantage, and a right to whatever God has provided. This means that you have the right and privilege to be healed and prosperous in all areas of your life. This means you have the right to use the name of Jesus to put the devil under your feet where he belongs. Sounds good doesn't it? An undeserved privilege means that you don't work for it, it is given to you. I paused and meditated on this scripture for 10 minutes and I will advise you to do the same. Jesus has brought you to a place of favour, wealth and abundance simply because of your faith in Him. Let me add that having faith in Christ means that

35

you simply trust in His finished work and the effect of that work. This, however, does not mean that you don't pray, fast, study the word of God, win souls and go to church. These things are good and help build you up spiritually, but they can be mere activities if you don't understand what Jesus has done for you. Many people pray and fast and do all sorts of things to be blessed and do not realise that they are already blessed.

Anything anyone does for the Lord must be born out of a relationship with Him and done in faith that is based on Jesus finished work, not your own effort. Do not ever think that you have a right with God because you are good. NO, God made you righteous through Jesus Christ.

The book of Colossians 1:12 says, **"Giving thanks unto the Father, which hath made us meet (qualified or enabled us) to be partakers of the inheritance of the saints in light"**. This is what the Spirit of God said to me and I just got so excited and took communion as soon as He said it. The word *partaker* in its simplest meaning is broken down like this: *Part* means you have a part; *Taker* means someone who takes. Just in case you don't understand what I mean, in other words, your part is to take. I said, "YES, LORD, I AM GOING TO TAKE ALL THAT YOU HAVE PROVIDED!"

Get rid of that unworthy mentality. It is an insult to Jesus when you deprive Him of extending His goodness to you by speaking unworthy words. Imagine if as a father, you left your children a good inheritance of a house, £1 million, and properties in different countries, and they said to you, "Oh, we can't have that; it's too much for us. We don't deserve it." How would you feel as a father? I don't know about you, but I would probably slap some sense into them and say, **"Children, it's yours. You didn't work for it, but I did and I am giving it to you because by the reason of having**

being born into my family and having my name, you qualify for it. My blood runs through your veins."

You are a member of the household of God. According to Ephesians 2:19, Jesus Christ has qualified you and brought you to the place of undeserved favour and abundance, and He has qualified you to take every part of God's provision because He paid for it with His blood. You have His name as a born again child of God. Therefore, go to your Father's throne of grace in prayer and receive your healing, your children, your job, or your right to remain in the country. Receive it because based on the word of God, you have the right to it, it is your inheritance.

You Are Not Forgotten

Isaiah 49:15-16

"Can a mother forget the baby at her breast and have no compassion on the child she has borne? Though she may forget, I will not forget you! See, I have engraved you on the palms of my hands; your walls are ever before me."

Are you currently in a situation that seems unfair and looks like God has forgotten you? If this is how you feel, keep on reading, as I have some good news for you.

In life, we all go through unfair situations. Things happen to us that we do not understand and that are beyond our control. For some of you reading this, maybe you have lost someone who was close to you and you wonder why this is happening. Some of you reading this may have lost your job, business etc. My admonition to you is that when things happen and you do not understand why, this is when your faith needs to be stronger. In life, our faith will be tested. James 1:2-3 tells us, " **Consider it all joy, my brethren, when you encounter various trials, knowing that the testing of your faith produces endurance."** As I mentioned earlier, things will happen that will shake your faith, but in the midst of the storms of life, you can have joy. I know this is easier said than done but it is possible.

Joy in the midst of storms is possible because God is always there. Yes, He is. Psalm 34:18 says, " **The LORD is close to the broken-hearted and saves those who are crushed in spirit."** Jesus said in Luke 4:18 **"The Spirit of the Lord** *is*

upon me, because He hath anointed me to preach the gospel to the poor; He hath sent me to heal the broken-hearted." This is the good news that no matter how broken you are right now, no matter the hurts and the pains of life, Jesus was sent to heal you if only you will let Him into your life. The good news is that God never forgets His people. The opening scripture tells us that even if a mother forsakes her child, God will never forget His children because His children's pictures are engraved on the palms of His hands. Even if you are not a born again child of God and you are reading this, you still have hope because God is the one who created you and knows all about you. No matter how many poor decisions you have made, God can still do something with your life. You are engraved on God's hand which means that God can never go wrong with your life no matter the natural circumstances. In most cases, we are the ones who make wrong decisions though God might have been trying to warn us before. God can never go wrong with your life because He said in Jeremiah 29:11, "**For I know the plans I have for you," declares the** LORD, "**plans to prosper you and not to harm you, plans to give you hope and a future.**" God still has a plan for your life and His plans are good and filled with hope. God never forgets anyone no matter how astray they have gone. He always draws people close to Himself.

Let us see what David the Psalmist said in Psalm 139:

"**For You created my inmost being; You knit me together in my mother's womb. I praise You because I am fearfully and wonderfully made; Your works are wonderful, I know that full well. My frame was not hidden from You when I was made in the secret place, when I was woven together in the depths of the earth. Your eyes saw my unformed body; all the days ordained for me were written in your book before one** of them came to be. How precious to me are Your thoughts, God! How vast is the sum of them!"

Job also says in Job 7:17, **"What is mankind that you make so much of them, that you give them so much attention?"**

Can you see how much God really loves humankind? God cares for us so much that our days are written in His book. He gives us so much attention, and His plans for us are good. Well, you might think, "All of this sounds good but it is not for me." I tell you that if you say this is not for you then you are literally throwing away hope. This piece was written especially for you. God was so mindful of you that He got me to write this all because of you. God promised He will never leave us nor forsake us (Hebrews 13:5) and He promised us that, **"When you go through deep waters, I will be with you. When you go through rivers of difficulty, you will not drown. When you walk through the fire of oppression, you will not be burned up; the flames will not consume you."** (Isaiah 43:2)

Be encouraged today, for God has not forgotten you.

Who Are You, a Servant or a Son?

Hebrews 3:5-6

"Now Moses was faithful in all his house as a servant, for a testimony of those things which were to be spoken later; but Christ was faithful as a Son over His house— whose house we are, if we hold fast our confidence and the boast of our hope firm until the end."

The way you see yourself affects the way you relate to God the Father. For instance, if a child feels that their parents do not love them, they will do anything to buy their parents' love, and if that doesn't work, they give up on trying.

The scripture above says a lot about our relationship with God. The truth of the gospel is that not only did Jesus die for our sins, but He also changed the way we relate to God. Jesus said in Matthew 6:9, **"Pray like this: Our Father in heaven, may Your name be kept holy."**

He didn't start by saying, "O Most high God, creator of heaven and earth." NO, He said, "Our Father," though all the other things are good too and are worship to your Father.

The Bible says about Moses, who was an Old Testament figure, that he was a faithful *servant*, but Jesus, who is the New Testament figure, was faithful as a *Son*. Let me first ask, what is the difference between a servant and a son? A servant is someone who is employed for service only. The person will get paid their dues but that is as far as the

41

relationship can go. A servant has no say in any matter. A son, however, has a say in all the household matters. A son is in charge of his father's house. Consider this, I as a son of my father can enter my parents' room without feeling timid, but if I have a servant in my house and he or she should try that, may the Lord help such a person! Yes, my parents will feed all of us but when it comes to family matters, if we have a servant, such a person has no say.

Yes, God loves the servant because God is love, but there is no fruitful relationship. The relationship God had with Moses was limited. Every time God refers to Moses, God called him "my servant." God loved Moses and used him mightily; however, if Moses was to speak to New Testament believers, he would admit that we are more fortunate than he was. In fact, Jesus said in Matthew 11:11, **"Truly I say to you, among those born of women there has not arisen anyone greater than John the Baptist! Yet the one who is least in the kingdom of heaven is greater than he"** (New American Standard Bible). This means that someone who just got born again today is greater than all the prophets in the Old Testament and John the Baptist. What an honour!

The good news about Jesus is that Jesus is known as the Son of God, and Galatians 3:26 says, **"For you are all sons of God through faith in Christ Jesus."** As a new creation in Christ, you are a son or daughter of God. Let's look at Galatians 4:1-7 **"Now I say, as long as the heir is a child, he differeth nothing from a servant, though he be Lord of all; But is under tutors and governors until the time appointed by the father: So we also, when we were children, were serving under the elements of the world. But when the fullness of the time was come, God sent His Son, made of a woman, made under the law: That He might redeem them who were under the law: that we might receive the adoption of sons. And because you are** sons, God hath sent the Spirit of His Son into your hearts, crying: Abba, Father. Therefore, now he is not a servant, but a son. And if a son, an heir also through God." (KJV)

Children and servants are no different. When we were still children, most of the time, our parents related to us based on rules and regulations, though they loved us. But as time goes by and as you begin to mature into adulthood, wise parents relate to their children not on a set of rules but as part of a parental and adulthood relationship. Your parents do not need to give you set of rules because those rules are now embedded in your heart and they believe you are mature enough.

Likewise with God. God gave Israel rules because they were children. The Bible never calls them sons of Israel but children of Israel, but when the set time had come for God to change the way He relates to people, He sent forth His Son to redeem us and receive us as sons. As a new creation, you are a son and not a servant. John 1:12 says, **"But as many as received Him, to them gave He power to become the sons of God, even to them that believe on His name."** (KJV) As a born again child of God, you are a son of God.

43

How Do I Get Faith?

Romans 10:17

"So faith comes from hearing, that is, hearing the Good News about Christ."(NLT)

Many people know about the subject of faith. We know the definition of faith, and we know that it is impossible to please God without faith. We have heard so many times that we need faith for so many things, but a lot of people are frustrated because they do not know how to get faith. What a lot of people call faith is simply head knowledge or wishing. At times, you hear people say, " I wish God could do this for me." A lot of people have head faith- faith that acknowledges God can do anything but when it comes to themselves, they don't believe He can do anything for them. This is head faith and not faith that is rooted in God's word. So this leads me to ask the question, how do I get faith?

The scripture above says that faith comes from hearing the good news about Jesus Christ. This signifies that we have got to take heed of what we listen to. Every day, consciously listen to what you are listening to. Ask yourself, is what I am listening to the good news about Christ? The New Testament is about the good news of Jesus Christ. So then, what is the good news of Jesus Christ? The good news is, you are saved by grace (Ephesians 2:5). You are made the righteousness of God in Christ Jesus (1 Corinthians 5:21). God's love for you is found in Christ Jesus (Romans 8:39). You can live free from the bondage of sin (Romans 6:14). God supplies all of your needs (Philippians 4:19). Jesus Christ brought you to a place of undeserved privilege

44

(Romans 5:2). You are a member of God's family (Ephesians 2:22). God loves you and chose you before the foundation of the world (Ephesians 1:4). You are blessed with all spiritual blessing (Ephesians 1:3). You are forgiven (Ephesians 1:7). By the blood of Jesus, you have access to God the father (Ephesians 2:13). God is your father (Romans 8:14-18). You are a joint heir with Christ (Galatians 4:6-7). You are a partaker of God's nature (2 Peter 1:4). You are redeemed as kings and queens unto God and you reign on this earth through Jesus Christ (Revelations 5:10). All this and many more are the good news of what Jesus has done for you.

The Gospel

Romans 1:16-17

"For I am not ashamed of the gospel, for it is the power of God for salvation to everyone who believes, to the Jew first and also to the Greek. For in it the righteousness of God is revealed from faith to faith; as it is written, 'BUT THE RIGHTEOUS man SHALL LIVE BY FAITH.'"

I love this scripture so much. Paul speaks of the gospel of Jesus Christ. I asked myself, what is the gospel of Jesus Christ? The gospel of Jesus Christ is the gospel of GRACE. How do I know this? Acts 20:24, **"But none of these things move me, neither count I my life dear unto myself, so that I might finish my course with joy, and the ministry, which I have received of the Lord Jesus, to testify the gospel of the grace of God."**

What is grace? Grace in its simplest definition means the unmerited favour of God, or the divine assistance of God. This means that the good news of God's love, forgiveness, mercy and favour is the power of God to save anyone who chooses to believe. I was talking to a friend of mine and he told me about himself going out to evangelise and told someone, "God loves you." The person replied, "You just made my day!" His next-door neighbour bought a Bible and now wants to be born again because of the message of God's grace. The message of God's grace is the power of the gospel.

The next verse says, **"For in it the righteousness of God is revealed."** I took a long pause and meditated on this and asked myself, "What is righteousness?" Righteousness simply means God's way of making people right with Himself. The grace of God provided a way for us to be right with God. When people try to earn their way with God or score points with God, they fail miserably. Religion will tell you that you have to do certain things to be accepted by God, but the Bible teaches that to be accepted by God, all you have to do is accept His perfect gift and sacrifice, Jesus Christ. When you receive Jesus as your Lord and Saviour, you are made right with God, as it is written in God's word according to 2 Corinthians 5:21, **"For God made Christ, who never sinned, to be the offering for our sin, so that we could be made right with God through Christ."** The righteousness of God is revealed in Christ.

Finally, let us look at Romans 3:21-26, **"But now God has shown us a way to be made right with Him without keeping the requirements of the law, as was promised in the writings of Moses and the prophets long ago. We are made right with God by placing our faith in Jesus Christ. And this is true for everyone who believes, no matter who we are. For everyone has sinned; we all fall short of God's glorious standard. Yet God freely and graciously declares that we are righteous. He did this through Christ Jesus when He freed us from the penalty for our sins. For God presented Jesus as the sacrifice for sin. People are made right with God when they believe that Jesus sacrificed His life, shedding His blood. This sacrifice shows that God was being fair when He held back and did not punish those who sinned in times past, for He was looking ahead and including them in what He would do in this present time. God did this to demonstrate His righteousness, for He Himself is fair and just, and He declares sinners to be righteous in His sight when they believe in Jesus."**

God declares us right with Himself when we believe in our hearts and confess with our mouths that Jesus is Lord over our lives and that He paid the penalty for our sins. When we come to God based on what Jesus did for us, we are declared righteous. This is the righteousness of God that is revealed through grace.

The Righteousness of Faith

Romans 1:16-17
"But the righteous man shall live by faith."

When I read this I thought, "Who are the righteous? Faith in what?" Before I proceed, this scripture is not talking about the faith that comes by works. As you read further, you will understand what I mean.

If you are born again child of God, you are the righteous. Righteousness is not based on works; you are made righteous when you get born again. 2 Corinthians 5:21 says, **"For He** (God) **made Him** (Jesus) **who knew no sin to be sin for us, that we might become the righteousness of God in Him**." You don't earn righteousness, you are made right. As a born again child of God, you've been made right with God.

Now, the Bible says the righteous shall live by faith, so I asked, "Faith in what?" The Bible has the answer to every question. Galatians 2:20-21 says, **"And the life which I now live in the flesh I live by faith in the Son of God, who loved me and gave Himself for me. I do not set aside the grace of God; for if righteousness comes through the law, then Christ died in vain."**

This means that the life you live as a believer must primarily be based in Jesus, who loves you, gave Himself for you and made you right with God. Many people live by faith in themselves, their qualifications, or their wealth. Although these things are not bad in themselves, they will fail you.

49

Trusting in these things without God is called *pride of life* and if anyone has the pride of life, the love of the Father does not dwell in such person (1 John 2:16). The righteous shall also live in the truth that he has been made right with God. He/she must be convinced that they are the righteousness of God in Christ.

You might ask, how do I live by faith in the Son of God? If you are not yet born again, get born again. Then start by knowing Him by studying the Bible and familiarizing yourself with the scriptures.

Finally, as a person who has been made right, base your faith on God's love for you, His word, and His way of doing things. As you do this, you will learn to live by faith.

The Witness of the Holy Spirit

Romans 8:16

"The Spirit Himself bears witness with our spirit that we are children of God."

What does it mean to bear witness? To bear witness simply means to confirm that something is true. In other words, what the scripture tells us is that part of the work of the Holy Spirit is to confirm that you are a child of God. When you become born again, the Holy Spirit comes to reside inside of you. His ministry is to convict people of their sin and their rightness with God. There are people who feel like they are born again one day and a sinner another day. God knew this would happen and that is why He put the scripture there. The Holy Spirit will always remind you of your position in Christ so that you can live a victorious Christian life.

This is why it is important that as believers; we do not quench the voice of the Holy Spirit. When you quench His voice, you will be open to the lies and deception of the enemy. The Bible warns us in Hebrews 3:8, "**Today, if you will hear His voice, do not harden your hearts.**" Why does it give us this warning? "**Beware, brethren, lest there be in any of you an evil heart of unbelief in departing from the living God; but exhort one another daily, while it is called 'Today,' lest any of you be hardened through the deceitfulness of sin.**" When you harden your heart, you become open to the deception of sin.

Brethren, be open to the reproof and direction of the Holy Spirit and when you miss it, do not condemn yourself, but repent and move on with Him. Even when you feel condemned, the best thing you can do for yourself is to stick to God's word and allow Him to help you. Listen to the voice that tells you, "You're still my son or daughter." The Bible says, **"There is therefore now no condemnation to those who belong to Christ who do not walk according to the flesh but the Spirit."** (Romans 8:1-2)

This means Christ does not condemn you, but your flesh does and if you yield to the Spirit of God, you will defeat condemnation.

Remain blessed.

You Are the Light of the World

Matthew 5:14

"You are the light of the world. A city set on a hill cannot be hidden."

I was at work one day, securing an entrance outside of the venue. The place was really dark and I was alone but not lonely. I was pondering on scriptures in the dark and suddenly from the corner of my eyes; I could see a shining light from a distance. I thought to myself, "I wish I had light here," and suddenly a scripture arose within me, "YOU ARE THE LIGHT OF THE WORLD." I wanted to scream but I held my peace.

People of God what am I saying? In this dark world, you are the light. This world is full of darkness, but in the midst of the darkness, there is a light. What does light do? It shows people the way and helps people to see. People are in deep darkness and do not know where they are going and what they are doing, so your duty is to show the way and introduce them to the source of the light, JESUS.

Anywhere you are, have the mind-set that you are the light. I didn't say that you are the light, Jesus did. Jesus is the source of the light according to John 8:12, and He said that you are the light. Jesus went further to say that you must let your light shine brightly. This means do not hide the light in you, let it shine. Tell somebody about Jesus, bless people with your resources, encourage others, give people phone calls, excel in your endeavours, pray for others, give out tracts, let the word of God in you control you. Let your light shine so that men may see your good works and glorify your father in heaven.

When people see the light in you, they will want to know more about Jesus. When people see the joy in you, and the peace in you, they want to know what keeps you smiling. I was talking to a sister few days ago and she said, "You don't need a lot to be joyful, you just need God." If the people of the world see your joy, they will want it. Paul said in Philippians 2:15, **"So that you may become blameless and pure, children of God without fault in a crooked and depraved generation, in which you shine like stars in the universe."** You are a shining star. A star shines even in the night, so as a child of light, shine in the dark.

Be of good courage today.

"Arise, shine; for thy light is come, and the glory of the LORD is risen upon thee. For, behold, the darkness shall cover the earth, and gross darkness the people: but the LORD shall arise upon thee, and his glory shall be seen upon thee. And the Gentiles shall come to thy light, and kings to the brightness of thy rising." (Isaiah 60:1-3).

Keep Your Eyes on Jesus

Hebrews 12:2

"Looking away [from all that will distract] to Jesus, Who is the Leader and the Source of our faith." (AMP)

"We do this by keeping our eyes on Jesus, the champion who initiates and perfects our faith." (NLT)

In the world we live in, there are so many things that call for our attention. The media is constantly exposing people to things such as nudity, drugs, and all sorts of filthy things. Yes, through the media we are also exposed to the things of God, but mainly we are exposed to filthiness. We can easily get distracted by so many things, but we children of light are to look away from these things by looking unto Jesus and keeping our entire being focused on Him entirely.

A lot of people claim to look unto Jesus but are still listening to worldly music such has R&B. Music has the power to restore or destroy our soul. What you fill your mind with will eventually affect the way you think and then your actions. Little distractions from the world can hinder our walk with God. For instance, you cannot claim to be a Christian, yet be found in the club or watching TV all day and only studying your Bible once a week.

To stay away from these worldly distractions, you need to look unto Jesus. Find out what Jesus wants you to do. Jesus said, **"What good is it if you gain the whole world and lose your soul?"** I believe this scripture does not only talk

55

about money but every distraction the world has to offer. The scripture tells us in 1 John 2:16-17, **"For all that is in the world—the lust of the flesh [craving for sensual gratification] and the lust of the eyes [greedy longings of the mind] and the pride of life [assurance in one's own resources or in the stability of earthly things]—these do not come from the Father but are from the world [itself.]"** These things that the world offers will distract you from God.

Young people have much temptation. You have the temptation from friends who invite you to wild parties, temptation to have sex with the opposite gender, to fight, take drugs etc. Look away from these distractions and focus on your walk with Christ. People will challenge your faith but you must remain focused. Your friends will mock you, but remain focused. God will help you if you remain focused on Him. Keep Jesus in the centre of your heart.

Once you know your worth in Christ, you will be unstoppable. The only thing that can stop you is yourself. Once Christ is the centre of your life, you become the centre of attraction to your generation. A lot of youths in our generation have what it takes to be the leaders of tomorrow, but only few recognise it.

Change your mind today, ask God what it is you need to change and He will show you in His word. Have the courage to change and God will help.

Restoration of God's Divine Favour

2 Corinthians 5:19

"It was God [personally present] in Christ, reconciling *and* restoring the world to favour with Himself, not counting up *and* holding against [men] their trespasses [but cancelling them], and committing to us the message of reconciliation (of the restoration to favour)."(Amplified Version)

Praise the Lord my beloved,

Most favoured people of God, I am so excited about what God is doing in my life and your lives. I thank God for what He has done in the past, what He is doing now, but most importantly, I am thankful for what He is going to do very soon in my life and yours.

Brethren, did you know that when Christ died on the cross, one of the things He purchased by His blood is your favour? Did you know that as a born again believer, by right, the favour of God belongs to you?

If you didn't know, I'm telling you now: God's favour belongs to you. "Oh brother Ade, you can't be serious," you say. "I mean look at me, why should God favour someone like me?" Let me tell you this, number 1: you are His child if you are born again and number 2: it's not all about what you've done; it's all about what Jesus did. The scripture above shows us that whilst Christ was here, God was with Him, reconciling us back to favour with Himself. When God favours you, everything begins to work for your good. When

57

Jesus died, with His blood He purchased your favour. You are not an average person, but you are divinely favoured and that is why I am so sure that before this week rounds up, God will surprise you.

God is full of surprises. He surprised the devil by making him think that mankind is doomed. You may not look favoured now but the truth is, favour belongs to you. Paul said in 2 Corinthians 9:8 **"And God is able to make all grace (every favour and earthly blessing) come to you in abundance."** God can cause people to favour you, your children, your business and all that concerns you. I should have titled this message *abundant favour.* God can cause abundant favour to abound towards you if only you believe and give toward His kingdom cheerfully because abundant favour is yours in Christ.

The Bible tells us in 2 Corinthians 5:17, **"Therefore, if anyone *is* in Christ, *he is* a new creation; old things have passed away; behold all things have become new."** This means that when you come to Christ, your past is written off. God no longer holds any charges against you. This means that He makes you free on the inside. Your life begins to take on a new course. The scripture also tell us in Romans 3:29, **"And now that you belong to Christ, you are the true children of Abraham. You are his heirs, and God's promise to Abraham belongs to you."** What did God promise Abraham? Genesis 12:2, **"And I will make of you a great nation, and I will bless you [with abundant increase of favours] and make your name famous *and* distinguished, and you will be a blessing [dispensing good to others]."** That is your portion the moment you give your life to Christ. Abundant favour becomes yours.

You are blessed in Jesus' name.

Praise, The Key to Unlimited Miracles

Mathew 14:18

"Taking the five loaves and the two fish and looking up to heaven, *He gave thanks* and broke the loaves. Then He gave them to the people. They all ate and were satisfied, and the disciples picked up twelve basketfuls of broken pieces that were left over."

I was meditating on Kenneth Copeland's broadcast in which he spoke about watching our mouth and he said something that caught my attention. "If you want anything in God's kingdom, you sow for it." Suddenly it dawned on me that if I want unlimited miracles in my life, I must give thanks to God for them first, sow material and spiritual seeds towards them, and I shall have what I believe. In the 14th chapter of Matthew verse 18, God gave me an example. There was a shortage of food, however Jesus took the five loaves of bread and two fishes, lifted them up to God, and gave thanks. What was the result of that? Multiplication. Jesus knew that for His seed to multiply, and for Him to have victory, He needed to give thanks first.

Friend, if you want miracles in your life, praise precedes victory. Thank God even before you receive it. Bless God for what you have, but praise Him ahead for the things to come. Jesus gave us a great example in the gospel of Matthew 14:18.

However, there is one thing we must avoid at all cost, negative words. Jesus said in Mark 11:23 that you shall have what you say. When you praise God, speak the right words

59

because your words create your world. Avoid negative words. Don't thank God for a miracle job then start saying that it's hard to get a job. Remember the word of the Lord that says in Ecclesiastes 5:6, **"Suffer not thy mouth to cause thy flesh to sin; neither say thou before the angel, that it was an error: wherefore should God be angry at thy voice, and destroy the work of thine hands?"**

Brethren, praise precedes victory but do not let the same mouth that praises God cause you to sin. Today marks a new beginning for you. Praise God ahead of time, speak God's word concerning what you praise for, sow both materially and spiritually for want you want and see the miracle working God work in your life.

Overcoming Discouragement

Nehemiah 8:10

"Don't be dejected and sad, for the joy of the LORD is your strength!"

Every time the people of God step out in faith to do God's will, the enemy always brings opposition to distract the people of God. I will show you this from the scriptures. Revelations 12:17 says, **"And he (Satan) went to make war with the rest of her offspring, who keep the commandments of God and have the testimony of Jesus Christ."**

Every believer is involved in spiritual warfare because they have the testimony of Jesus Christ. The Bible says in Ephesians 6:10-12 **"Finally, my brethren, be strong in the Lord and in the power of His might. Put on the whole armour of God, that you may be able to stand against the wiles of the devil. For we do not wrestle against flesh and blood, but against principalities, against powers, against the rulers of the darkness of this age, against spiritual hosts of wickedness in the heavenly places."** Our warfare is not physical but spiritual and one of the devices the enemy uses to make war with the people of God is discouragement. To be discouraged means to be oppressed, distressed, or frustrated about something. This is why Paul admonishes us in 2 Corinthians 2:11 that for the enemy not to outwit us, we must not be ignorant of his devices or evil schemes. Discouragement can come in many forms such as false accusations, mockery, scoffing, just to frustrate the people of God. Let us look at a few instances in
61

which the enemy brought discouragement to the people of God.

The book of Ezra chapter 3:1-2 tells us that:

"In early autumn, when the Israelites had settled in their towns, all the people assembled in Jerusalem with a unified purpose. Then Jeshua son of Jehozadak joined his fellow priests and Zerubbabel son of Shealtiel with his family in rebuilding the altar of the God of Israel." Here we can see that the Israelites stepped out in faith to start rebuilding the altar of God which had been destroyed.

Now Ezra 4:1-5, 24 tells us that, "The enemies of Judah and Benjamin heard that the exiles were rebuilding a Temple to the Lord, the God of Israel. So they approached Zerubbabel and the other leaders and said, "Let us build with you, for we worship your God just as you do. We have sacrificed to Him ever since King Esarhaddon of Assyria brought us here." But Zerubbabel, Jeshua, and the other leaders of Israel replied, 'You may have no part in this work. We alone will build the Temple for the Lord, the God of Israel, just as King Cyrus of Persia commanded us.' Then the local residents tried to discourage and frighten the people of Judah to keep them from their work. They bribed agents to work against them and to frustrate their plans. This went on during the entire reign of King Cyrus of Persia and lasted until King Darius of Persia took the throne. So the work on the Temple of God in Jerusalem had stopped, and it remained at a standstill until the second year of the reign of King Darius of Persia." (NLT)

Another story of how the enemy seeks to frustrate God's people is found in Nehemiah. In those days, Nehemiah was the king's cupbearer. News came to Nehemiah that the walls of Jerusalem had been destroyed with fire and his people were distressed. Nehemiah was saddened by this news. However, to go and oversee what was happening and step out to God's work, he needed the king's permission, which was granted unto him by the grace of God.

Nehemiah set out on his journey to Jerusalem and within three days of his arrival, he began to inspect the walls in which time I believe he was receiving inspiration from God as to how he would go on about rebuilding the wall. After surveying the wall, Nehemiah told the officials, "**You know very well what trouble we are in. Jerusalem lies in ruins, and its gates have been destroyed by fire. Let us rebuild the wall of Jerusalem and end this disgrace!**' Then I told them about how the gracious hand of God had been on me, and about my conversation with the king. They replied at once, 'Yes, let's rebuild the wall!' So they began the good work** (Nehemiah 2:18). Now, it looks like all is going well and rosy but verse 19 says, "**But when Sanballat, Tobiah, and Geshem the Arab heard of our plan, they scoffed contemptuously. 'What are you doing? Are you rebelling against the king?' they asked. I replied, "The God of heaven will help us succeed. We, His servants, will start rebuilding this wall. But you have no share, legal right, or historic claim in Jerusalem."**

Nehemiah 4:1-3, "**Sanballat was very angry when he learned that we were rebuilding the wall. He flew into a rage and mocked the Jews, saying in front of his friends and the Samarian army officers, 'What does this bunch of poor, feeble Jews think they're doing? Do they think they can build the wall in a single day by just offering a few sacrifices? Do they actually think they can make something of stones from a rubbish heap—and charred ones at that?' Tobiah the Ammonite, who was standing**

beside him, remarked, 'That stone wall would collapse if even a fox walked along the top of it.'

The above scriptures give us a little insight on how the enemy can bring discouragement if the people of God permit him to. Anybody that steps out in faith to do God's work will always have opportunity to be discouraged. As you study more about Nehemiah, you will see more about the plan of Judah's enemy to frustrate the work of God. Even though the temple was eventually built, there was a shortage of food, people were complaining of not having enough money to buy food, they were charged high interest on what they borrowed, and the list goes on and on. Nehemiah eventually got frustrated, but God gave him wisdom to overcome.

Now that we have discovered the enemies' strategy to distract us, how can we silence him? Praise

Praise

Psalm 8:2

"Out of the mouth of babes and nursing infants, You have ordained strength, because of Your enemies, that You may silence the enemy (Satan) and the avenger."

In the midst of all that could go wrong, when you are discouraged, praise God. Praise silences the voice of Satan. Isaiah 61:3 shows that one of the ministries of the Holy Spirit is to give us the garment of praise for the spirit of heaviness: " **To console those who mourn in Zion, to give them beauty for ashes, the oil of joy for mourning, the garment of praise for the spirit of heaviness."** Praise destroys heaviness. Paul said in Hebrews 12:2-3, "**Looking away [from all that will distract] to Jesus, Who is the Leader and the Source of our faith [giving the first incentive for our belief] and is also its Finisher [bringing it to maturity and perfection]. He, for the joy [of obtaining the prize] that was set before Him, endured the cross, despising and ignoring the shame, and is now seated at the right hand of the throne of God. Just think of Him Who endured from sinners such grievous opposition and bitter hostility against Himself [reckon up and consider it all in comparison with your trials], so that you may not grow weary or exhausted, losing heart and relaxing and fainting in your minds."**

To look away from discouragement, focus on Jesus, praise God and ignite that joy of the Lord in you. Just as the scripture says in Nehemiah 8:10, **"Don't be dejected and sad, for the joy of the LORD is your strength!"**

When you maintain your joy, you are full of strength, and strength is the ability to keep moving forward in the midst of hardship. I love what Jesus said to His disciples: **"God blesses you when people mock you and persecute you and lie about you and say all sorts of evil things against you because you are my followers. Be happy about it! Be very glad! For a great reward awaits you in heaven. And remember, the ancient prophets were persecuted in the same way."**

Therefore, rejoice, rejoice, and keep rejoicing.

What Are You Saying?

Matthew 17:20

"You don't have enough faith," Jesus told them. "I tell you the truth, if you had faith even as small as a mustard seed, you could say to this mountain, 'Move from here to there,' and it would move. Nothing would be impossible."

If you have faith..., you can say...

The reason why many are not experiencing the blessings God has for them is not because God doesn't want to give to them, it's not because they don't believe, but it's because they do not say what they believe. If you truly believe what God says about you, you will declare it. 2 Corinthians 4:13 says, **"We having the same spirit of faith, according as it is written, I believed, and therefore have I spoken; we also believe, and therefore speak."** Speak what you believe. We have heard many times that our words bring life, therefore if you want life, speak the word of life. Paul said that we have believed, and therefore speak. Faith speaks. If you believe in Jesus, speak about Him.

A man of God (Bishop David Oyedepo) says that a closed mouth is a closed destiny. So if you do not speak forth the word into your life, you close your destiny. What you speak matters a lot, so speak the word of God. David Oyedepo saw from God's word that he can never be poor so he screamed, "I can never be poor!" and now God has confirmed that in his life.

Other reasons why believers don't experience God's best is not because they do not speak, but because they don't have faith in what they speak. Confessing God's word is good; however, it's no use if there is no faith. Jesus said in Mark 11:23, **"For verily I say unto you, that whosoever shall say unto this mountain, 'Be thou removed, and be thou cast into the sea'; and shall not DOUBT IN HIS HEART, BUT SHALL BELIEVE that those things which he saith shall come to pass; he shall have whatsoever he saith."** Confessing the word isn't enough, faith in what you say is what matters.

So, let me ask you again, what are you saying concerning your life? Jesus said in Matthew 12:34, **"Out of the abundance of the heart the mouth speaks."** That which is in your heart sets the pace for your words. So I challenge you today, speak God's word and not only that, believe in it. Jesus said that if you speak in faith, act on it, and believe in it, then you shall have what you say. Watch what you say because it will determine the course of your life.

The Goodness of God

Psalm 106:1

"Praise the LORD! Oh give thanks to the LORD, for He is good, for His steadfast love endures forever."

There are many things God has done for us that we ought to thank Him for. A man of God said, "If you think well, you can thank well." The fact that you are able to think is worth giving God thanks for. You might say, "Nothing is working for me." The fact that you still have eyes to see and hears to hear and a mouth to talk and they all work is worth giving thanks for. The fact that you and I are alive today is part of the goodness of God.

God is a good God. David said in Psalm 124:2-3 that if the LORD had not been on their side when men attacked them, when their anger flared against them, they would have swallowed them alive. Friend, you can agree with me that if God had not preserved you, you would have been wiped out by Satan. If God had not kept you during your sleep, you could have died. If God had not guarded your footsteps, men will have attacked you; David said that He who keeps Israel neither slumber nor sleeps. This means that God watches us 24/7, protecting us and caring for us, so isn't He worthy of thanks?

As a parent, you can't always be there with your children, and God has been so good to you by keeping your children alive. God has been so good to us. Many are dead, but we are still alive. Many are in hunger, but God feeds us. Many are in need of a saviour, but we have one. If it wasn't for the goodness of God, we would not be here today.

I was worshiping one day and I remembered this song:

"I have seen the Lord's goodness; His mercy and compassion,

I have seen the Lord's goodness, Hallelujah, praise the Lord!

O Lord you have been so good to me,

O Lord you are excellent in my life every day."

Another says:

"Thank you Jesus,

Thank you my Lord,

Wherever I am now,

It is by your grace. "

Paul said in 1 Corinthians 15:10, "But by the grace of God I am what I am, and His grace to me was not without effect. No, I worked harder than all of them—yet not I, but the grace of God that was with me."

The grace of God is what is keeping you, so give thanks to Him for He is good and His mercy endures forever.

Partakers of Inheritance

Colossians 1:12

"Giving thanks to the Father who has qualified us to be partakers of the inheritance of the saints in the light."

Every earthly father either has or wishes to give their children an inheritance materially even though the greatest inheritance to give your children is Christ. No parent in their right state of mind wishes their children to suffer. Jesus said in Matthew 7:9, **"Or what man is there among you who, if his son asks for bread, will give him a stone? Or if he asks for a fish, will he give him a serpent? If you then, being evil, know how to give good gifts to your children, how much more will your Father who is in heaven give good things to those who ask Him!"**

And in Luke 12:32, **"Fear not, little flock; for it is your Father's good pleasure to give you the kingdom."**

It's God's delight to give you all that He has spiritually and materially. God is your father and it does not give Him pleasure to see His people always broke, or in sickness. Yes, you will go through trials but Psalm 34:19 says, **"A righteous man may have many troubles, but the LORD delivers him from them all."** This means your troubles are but for a moment and not a lifetime. God does not take pleasure in your being broke. Psalm 35:27 says, **"Let them shout for joy and rejoice, who favour my vindication, and let them say continually, 'The LORD be magnified, Who delights in the prosperity of His servant.'"**

71

You have an inheritance in Christ. You did not qualify for it, but as the scripture says, God qualified you- meaning He made you worthy of it. Through the death of Christ and by your accepting what Jesus has done for you, God gave you an inheritance. Ephesians 1:11 says, **"Furthermore, because we are united with Christ, we have received an inheritance from God, for He chose us in advance, and He makes everything work out according to His plan."**

As a child of God, He gave you rights to the things of His kingdom. You have the right to be healed, be blessed materially, be full of joy, and have a sound mind. Everything God has, He gave it to you. If you don't have it, it's not God's fault. God's word is God's will for you. God has everything prepared, but it's up to you to believe and receive it by faith. You can have a healthy relationship with God, and be blessed in all things including material things. The blessings of Abraham were not just spiritual blessings, but material blessing too. All the men of God were blessed in all things. Paul was a blessed man: though He might not have been rich in money, the man was blessed materially because he had Christ. Christ provided for him when he was hungry, and Paul was also a giver though he wasn't as blessed as other men. Jesus ensured His disciples lacked nothing. Luke 22:35, **"Then Jesus asked them, 'When I sent you without purse, bag or sandals, did you lack anything?'**

'Nothing,' they answered."

If you are a born again child of God, you have the right to claim what God has provided for you in His Word. You do not deserve anything from God, but because God is good, He has made you a partaker of His inheritance in Christ Jesus. You have the right to receive anything God wants for you. The problem with many believers is that they close their eyes to the word of God. They come begging God instead of opening their eyes to what God has for them and boldly and gladly receiving it by faith. How would you look if I told you that the money in my account is yours, yet you are begging for it? Until you understand the grace of God, you can never understand who God is and what He has given you as His child. If you believe then you are the seed of Abraham.

Galatians 3:29 says, **"And now that you belong to Christ, you are the true children of Abraham. You are his heirs, and God's promise to Abraham belongs to you."**

What is the promise of Abraham? Genesis 12:2-3, **"And I will make of you a great nation, and I will bless you [with abundant increase of favours] and make your name famous and distinguished, and you will be a blessing [dispensing good to others]. And I will bless those who bless you [who confer prosperity or happiness upon you] and [a]curse him who curses or uses insolent language toward you; in you will all the families and kindred of the earth be blessed [and by you they will bless themselves]."**

The Bible tells us in Genesis 24:1, **"Now Abraham was old, well advanced in years, and the Lord had blessed Abraham in all things."** ALL MEANS ALL WITH NOTHING LEFT OUT. Abraham was blessed materially.

Genesis 13:2, **"Now Abram was extremely rich in livestock and in silver and in gold."** Not only was he prosperous materially, but he lived in good health, was spiritually sound, and he was called a friend of God (James 2:23) as he had an intimate relationship with God, though he was materially rich.

God is your father, and He has an inheritance for you. An inheritance your mind cannot capture. It is up to you to receive it. Ephesians 2: 18 tells us, **"For through Him we**

73

both have access by one Spirit to the Father. Now, therefore, you are no longer strangers and foreigners, but fellow citizens with the saints and members of the household of God." Brethren, if you are a member of God's household, and if you have access to God, then you have access to all that He has and all the He is. Praise the Lord!

Be blessed of the Lord.

The Treasure Within

2 Corinthians 4:7

"But we have this treasure in earthen vessels, that the excellence of the power may be of God and not of us."

As believers, you and I carry a treasure within us. As I began to meditate on this scripture, I remembered the words of Jesus Christ in John 14:15-17, "**If you love me, keep my commands. And I will ask the Father, and He will give you another advocate to help you and be with you forever— the Spirit of truth. The world cannot accept Him, because it neither sees Him nor knows Him. But you know Him, for He lives with you and will be in you.**" This truth is powerful, that the very God who made the earth will come to live inside of you. The very day you gave your life to Christ, God came to dwell in you. God lives in you. This is the reason why you and I must be aware of his presence in us.

The apostle Paul prayed a prayer for the church at Ephesus. He said in Ephesians 3:19, "**...that you may be filled [through all your being] unto all the fullness of God [may have the richest measure of the divine Presence, and become a body wholly filled and flooded with God Himself.]**" Paul prayed that we should be filled with God Himself and the only way you and I can be filled with God Himself is by the indwelling of the Holy Ghost. When the Holy Spirit dwells in you, the Bible says that out of you shall flow rivers of living water. This means that He begins to touch others through you, people begin to see Christ in you,

75

and you become a unique being, because Christ in you is the hope of glory.

Jesus lives in you because of the Holy Spirit and because Jesus lives in you, Paul says in 1 Corinthians 2:16, **"You have the mind of Christ."** This means you think the way Christ thinks, you speak the way He speaks; Christ dominates you.

Friend, that is the power you and I carry in us— the God of the universe Himself. I didn't say it, the Bible did. Paul said in 1 Corinthians 6:19, **"Do you not know that your bodies are temples of the Holy Spirit, who is in you, whom you have received from God? You are not your own."**

Finally, because the Spirit of God lives in you, you can pray more effectively. Paul said in Romans 8:26-27, **"We do not know what we ought to pray for, but the Spirit Himself intercedes for us through wordless groans. And He who searches our hearts knows the mind of the Spirit, because the Spirit intercedes for God's people in accordance with the will of God."** When you pray in the Spirit, you are talking to God directly, you speak in mysteries and you are praying according to the will of God for your life. This is why you need Him.

I pray that you are blessed by this and remain ever blessed.

Be Patient After Placing Your Order

Hebrews 6:10, 15

10- "We do not want you to become lazy, but to imitate those who through faith and patience inherit what has been promised." 15- "And so after waiting patiently, Abraham received what was promised."

Most times, I place an order on free items from KCM ministries and Joel Osteen ministries. Every time I see their letters I get excited because an opportunity is open before me to receive spiritual insight and place an order, and the most exciting thing is that the items ordered are guaranteed to be delivered.

However, after placing the order, the next stage is for me to wait. The question is, what do I do whilst waiting? Go on with my daily activities such as going to work. Also whilst waiting, I am always expecting a letter or package from the post. Whilst waiting, I am building patience, and increasing my expectation that today I will receive a letter or package.

Likewise with God. You have gone to His word, you have placed an order on what you need, God sends you a letter of acknowledgement by giving you peace of mind, and now the next process is to wait patiently for your order to be delivered. When I say wait, I don't mean do nothing. Whilst waiting, keep serving God knowing your package will be guaranteed. During the process of waiting, spend time in His word and develop your faith and patience. Many times, we read that scripture that says we should imitate those who through faith and patience inherit the promise, we miss out the patience bit but concentrate on faith. Many messages have been preached on faith but not many on patience. Patience and faith go together. In fact, patience is one of the fruits of the Spirit. When you are patient, your faith develops.

My encouragement to all of us is that we should all learn to be patient. Abraham waited 25 years and at the end he got the promise. After God told him he would have a son, Abraham didn't cross his legs and relax, but instead he continued serving God with patience, knowing that God is able to do what He said He will do.

Message of the Kingdom

Mark 1:14-15

"Now after John was put in prison, Jesus came to Galilee, preaching the gospel of the kingdom of God, and saying, 'The time is fulfilled, and the kingdom of God is at hand. Repent, and believe in the gospel.'"

One Friday, I went for fellowship meeting and it was awesome. The person who held the meeting used this scripture for the word and life was ministered to me. I went home thinking of the word that had been spoken and still am. I meditated on it so much that I asked the Holy Ghost to further my understanding of this scripture, and He did.

Today, I would like to share with you what I learnt: The message of the kingdom. The scripture says that Jesus was preaching the gospel of the kingdom and I paused and asked, what is the gospel of the kingdom? "Repent and believe." Yes, that is right but what are we supposed to repent and believe?" Jesus died for us." Yes, that is true but that is not all of it. A lot of people believe Jesus died for them but still haven't repented. After the fact that Jesus died for us, what else are we to believe and what is this gospel of the kingdom?

Isaiah 61:1 says, **"The Spirit of the Sovereign Lord is upon me, for the Lord has anointed me to bring good news to the poor. He has sent me to comfort the broken-hearted and to proclaim that captives will be released and prisoners will be freed."**

79

What is the gospel to the poor? Whatever is missing in your life can be fixed just by believing in the gospel. When people see the word "poor", money is the first thing that comes to mind. A lot of people are rich financially but are poor in other areas of their lives. You can be rich financially and be poor in relationships or in your health. You can have good relationships but lack finances. Any area in your life that is deficient shows that you are poor in that area, but Jesus can fix it if you believe.

Jesus was also preaching the gospel of physical, spiritual and emotional healing. He preached that whatever area in your life that needs healing can be touched. Jesus also preached liberty to the captives. This means you and I can be set free from anything that is binding us.

Isaiah 62:1-3 is the message of the kingdom. That passage is summed up in one word, DELIVERANCE.

According to Ephesians 2:17, Jesus also came to preach peace. The gospel of the kingdom is the gospel of peace.

The problem with most believers is this: when we see the word repent, we automatically think of sinners. Repentance is also for believers. Many so-called believers believe and have not repented. They know about Christ but the message of the kingdom has not been mixed with faith, therefore it profits them nothing. The gospel is simple, but for many of us it is hard to believe. For example, deliverance comes by taking the communion. It's simple, yet people find it hard to believe. Paul said in 2 Corinthians 11:3, **"But I fear, lest somehow, as the serpent deceived Eve by his craftiness, so your minds be corrupted from the simplicity that is in Christ."** The gospel is simple, yet because of deception, even believers find it hard to believe in the gospel. Jesus is saying now, "Repent and believe in the whole gospel, not half. Believe in the message of the Kingdom of God."

God bless you.

The Ministry of Jesus Christ and the Holy Spirit

Dear Brethren

I have been studying the book of Romans in chapter 8 for quite some time and, as I began to meditate on the scriptures, I asked the Holy Spirit to help to show me His ministry in Romans 8. As I began to read, verses 26-27 and 34 all of a sudden became alive in my spirit. I began to rejoice in my spirit because He quickened my understanding on how important He is in my life. Brethren, we need the Holy Spirit because He is vital to our prayer life. I learnt, by the help of God, to depend on the Holy Ghost in prayer. I do not just mean speaking in tongues, although that is a part of it, but I learnt to depend on Him even when praying for others. It's sweet fellowshipping with Him. He makes me want to study the word more.

Now, let us get into the word. I know you are familiar with this scripture, but I want you to open up because familiarity kills. If we get too familiar with a scripture, we can never get to see what God is saying. So please open up. Romans 8:26 says, **"For we do not know what we should pray for as we ought, but the Spirit Himself makes intercession for us."**

I have read this many times but never really saw it. The Holy Spirit said to me, "I pray for you every day." I almost ran out of my room to scream! The ministry of the Spirit of God is to pray for us. How does He pray for us? **"With groanings which cannot be uttered."** Speaking in tongues is of vital necessity in prayers, because as the scripture says, sometimes we do not know what to pray for but when you switch to tongues, the Spirit intercedes for you. What gave me a shock wave, and I mean I exploded, was the next sentence: **"Now He who searches the hearts knows what the mind of the Spirit is, because *He makes intercession for the saints according to the will of God.*"**

Did you see that? The Spirit of God prays for you according to the will of God. When you pray in the Spirit, the Holy Spirit is praying the will of God for your life. We cannot see the full picture of God's will but He who searches the heart and knows the mind of the Spirit, reveals it to the Holy Spirit according to 1 Corinthians 2:10, **"But God has revealed them to us through His Spirit. For the Spirit searches all things, yes, the deep things of God. For what man knows the things of a man except the spirit of the man which is in him? Even so no one knows the things of God except the Spirit of God. Now we have received, not the spirit of the world, but the Spirit who is from God, that we might know the things that have been freely given to us by God."**

To back this up again, Jesus said in John 16:13, **"However, when He, the Spirit of truth, has come, He will guide you into all truth; and He shall show you things to come**."

How does the Spirit reveal to us the will of God? Through praying, and not just praying in your understanding, but in the Spirit. Praise God. Very deep right? Well I am not done yet.

You see, until you make the Holy Spirit your best friend, prayer becomes a burden. The Holy Ghost is the revealer of the secrets of God. You cannot do without Him. Look at verse 34 of Romans 8 and we will see how the Holy Spirit and Jesus work together. I was overwhelmed with joy when

I saw this. The verse says, **"Who is He who condemns? It is Christ who died, and furthermore is also risen, who is even at the right hand of God,** *who also makes intercession for us."*

Jesus is not in heaven crossing His legs and relaxing, no. Jesus is constantly praying for you and me according to the will of God the father, praise God. Isn't that overwhelming that you are not alone in prayer? The Holy Spirit and Jesus praying for you doesn't take away the responsibility of you praying for yourself, however there is greater power when you pray with the Spirit in the name of Jesus. There is power released when you pray with those two forces. Also notice, three times the same scripture mentions that the heavenly being intercedes for us. This means that we have the power to withstand anything. No wonder Paul says, "If God be for us, who can be against us." God is for you, brethren, and remember: the Spirit of God, and God the Son, intercede for you daily and that is why I am assured that you and I cannot miss the will of God for our lives.

Finally, if Jesus and the Spirit intercede for us, we ought to do the same for others.

Remain in His love.

All of God's Promises are Fulfilled in Christ

2 Corinthians 1:20

"For as many as are the promises of God, they all find their Yes [answer] in Him [Christ]."

One thing about life is that sometimes it tries to beat us down. We all face unfair situations, and sometimes disappointments. We feel all washed up, but the only thing that keeps us encouraged through difficult situations is the word of God. For every situation, God has a promise.

Some people reading this: maybe you're looking for a future partner and you have been rejected by many. Do not give up, for the Bible says in Psalm 68:6, **"God places the lonely into a family,"** and He also said in Isaiah 34:16, **"None shall want her mate."** Some of you reading this are looking for children. God's word says in Exodus 23:25, **"You shall serve the Lord thy God and He shall bless your bread and water and He shall take sickness away from you and none shall be barren."** Some of you are looking for jobs. Philippians 4:19 says, **"My God shall supply all of my needs according to His riches in glory in Christ."**

No matter how many people have said *no* to you, no matter how much rejection or hurt you have faced, one thing stands sure and that is the word of God in the Bible. No matter what you are going through right now, locate what the word of God says about it. If your parents reject you, Psalm 46 says, even if your father and mother forsake you, the Lord will take care of you.

You are destined for greatness, you will excel in your studies and everything God has called you to do, you will graduate with flying colours and you will become the person God has destined you to be. All of God's promises are yes and they are fulfilled in Christ.

I encourage you to keep hoping, trusting, and loving Him. Delight yourself in the Lord and watch Him fulfil those promises in your life.

Grace That Makes Great

1 Corinthians 15:10
"But by the grace of God I am what I am."

As I was meditating on how far God has brought me, I heard the voice of the Spirit saying, "This is the word of the LORD to Zerubbabel, saying, 'Not by might, nor by power, but by my Spirit,' said the LORD of hosts." All of a sudden this scripture became alive and I heard in my spirit, "You can never become greater than what the grace of God makes you. Grace is what makes great. Where effort cannot take you, the grace of God will take you there. What we believers need to understand is that nothing in the kingdom of God can be accomplished by skill or human effort, NO. You can never become your best except by the grace of God. Grace is the very person of God and the divine enablement of God that causes you to do things you naturally cannot do so without Him, you can do nothing.

Everything you are today is by grace. You were saved by grace, you live by grace, and you serve God by His grace, so everything is by His grace. Paul said, "By the grace of God I am what I am," which means you are who you are by grace. Never take the grace of God for granted because once it is withdrawn from you, then you are open to satanic forces.

Remember, you are who you are by His grace. Grace makes great and I see the grace of God colouring your destiny in Jesus' name.

Remain ever blessed.

Change Your Thinking

Romans 12:2

"And do not be conformed to this world, but be transformed by the renewing of your mind, that you may prove what *is* that good and acceptable and perfect will of God."

I believe this scripture is so vital and the reason for this is because it helps us to change our thinking. There are two ways of thinking, one is right and the other is wrong. The world's way of thinking is wrong, carnal and deadly. Let me help your break this down.

Every time you see the word, "DO NOT" please pay close attention to it. God says *do not* be conformed to this world. This means everything that concerns the world's system e.g. fashion, music, language, ways of getting money, the Babylonian system, anything without God in it, DO NOT CONFORM TO IT. This world's system is without God and without hope. It is selfish; a destroyer of life, anti-Christ and it will kill you. The Message translation says, **"Don't become so well-adjusted to your culture that you fit into it without even thinking. Instead, fix your attention on God."** One of the things that destroys the body of Christ is culture. People have become so used to their own culture that they embrace it as part of Christianity. Just because your culture embraces something does not make it Biblically right. This is what God was talking about when He said, "Do not be conformed to this world." The world's way of thinking and doing things is messed up, carnal and it is crashing. Romans 8:6 says, **"For to be carnally minded is**
88

death" and you will be shocked that he was talking to believers. In the days of Paul, there were carnally minded Christians. In 1 Corinthians 3, Paul writes, **"Dear brothers and sisters, when I was with you I couldn't talk to you as I would to spiritual people. I had to talk as though you belonged to this world or as though you were infants in the Christian life. I had to feed you with milk, not with solid food, because you weren't ready for anything stronger. And you still aren't ready, for you are still controlled by your sinful nature. You are jealous of one another and quarrel with each other. Doesn't that prove you are controlled by your sinful nature? Aren't you living like people of the world? When one of you says, 'I am a follower of Paul,' and another says, 'I follow Apollos,' aren't you acting just like people of the world?"**

These people were Christians, yet behaved carnally and we still have believers like that today.

This will help a lot of us reading this. God said in Revelations 3:15-16, **"I know your works, that you are neither cold nor hot. I could wish you were cold or hot. So then, because you are lukewarm, and neither cold nor hot, I will vomit you out of My mouth."**

Friend, there is nothing worse than a lukewarm Christian: People with one leg in church and another in the world. Such people are miserable and cannot enjoy God's best. Such people cannot enjoy sin because they know it is wrong, yet they cannot approach God because of the sin. If you are one of such reading this, Jesus is telling you now to choose whom you will serve.

On the other hand, there is a right way to think. The word says we must be transformed by renewing our minds or paying close attention to God. The New Living Translation says, **"But let God transform you into a new person by**

89

changing the way you think." When you let God transform your thinking via studying the Bible, your thinking becomes alive to Him. Instead of being carnally minded, you become spiritually minded, and Paul says in Romans 8:6 that to be spiritually minded *is* life and peace. God's way of thinking gives you life and peace.

My charge to you today is to allow Jesus to change your carnal way of thinking. It is possible to speak in tongues, pray and do all sorts of things and yet be carnal. Once you allow Jesus to change you inside out, it will give you peace. Praise God.

Paid in Full

Hebrews 9:13-14

"The blood of goats and bulls and the ashes of a heifer sprinkled on those who are ceremonially unclean sanctify them so that they are outwardly clean. How much more, then, will the blood of Christ, who through the eternal Spirit offered Himself unblemished to God, cleanse our consciences from acts that lead to death, so that we may serve the living God."

One thing I love about the Bible is that it deals with all areas of life including how to deal with the secret sin you have that nobody knows about. I have also observed that many people in the body of Christ have the desire to serve God but are sin conscious, therefore are timid in approaching God because they are ignorant of His word.

The Bible says that we should come to Him boldly, however that is impossible when you have a sinful conscience. When you are sin conscious, you cannot approach God appropriately, but when you are aware of what the blood has done for you, you can come to God with boldness. Hebrews 10:19 says, **"Brothers and sisters, we are not afraid to enter the Most Holy Room. We enter boldly because of the blood of Jesus."**

Once you come to God and partake of the Holy Communion which Jesus provided for the remission of sin, the blood cleanses your conscience and breaks any addictions you have. I know what I am talking about because I have been there. The blood has the power to put an end to every dead

91

work in your life. The blood cleanses you inside so you can approach God with boldness. Look at what John says so you can get a clearer understanding. 1 John 1:7 says, **"And the blood of Jesus Christ His Son cleanses us from all sin."** ALL MEANS ALL. The blood of Jesus cleanses from pornography, masturbation, lying, stealing and every other sin. Once you partake of the communion not just once, but all the time, and declare victory over that sin, you will win. The blood paid for it and the blood will win. Never ever think that you can never overcome whatever issue you are facing, the answer is in the blood of Jesus Christ. HALLELUJAH.

love,

Ademola

Remain blessed.

Abrahamic Covenant of Grace Part 1

Genesis 12:1-3

"Now [in Haran] the Lord said to Abram, 'Go for yourself [for your own advantage] away from your country, from your relatives and your father's house, to the land that I will show you. And I will make of you a great nation, and I will bless you [with abundant increase of favours] and make your name famous and distinguished, and you will be a blessing [dispensing good to others]. And I will bless those who bless you [who confer prosperity or happiness upon you] and [a]curse him who curses or uses insolent language toward you; in you will all the families and kindred of the earth be blessed [and by you they will bless themselves]."

First of all, as new creations in Christ, we understand from scriptures that **"If you belong to Christ [are in Him who is Abraham's seed], then you are Abraham's offspring and [spiritual] heirs according to the promise."** (Galatians 3:29) This means that as long as you are in Christ Jesus, you have the right to claim every promise that God made to Abraham. When God made those promises to Abraham, he had you and me in mind.

Secondly, from the above scripture, we see that when God makes a covenant with an individual, He makes it based on His own ability. For instance, if I promised to give you £100, I am giving it to you based on my own account and not yours. The covenant God made with Abraham is the covenant of Grace. Grace is simply the ability of God at work

93

in an individual to accomplish things. The first Gospel that was ever preached in history was the gospel of Grace as you can see when God spoke to Abraham. Notice that God said, "I will". Grace is based on God's capacity to get things done and not ours. Abraham didn't have anything to do with it and as a matter of fact, all Abraham did was believe God and God accounted it to him as righteousness (Genesis 15:6).

This Abrahamic covenant of Grace includes seven promises. The first promise that God said was, "**I will make you a great nation.**" What this means is that the grace of God has the capacity to turn a man into a nation. Remember, when God speaks He speaks based on His own ability. Abraham and his wife were barren but God was not looking at that. God saw nations, kings and queens coming out of the loins of a couple whose bodies were past the age of giving birth. Grace has no boundaries. The Grace of God knows no impossibilities. The Grace of God amplifies a man in the area of impossibilities. God said in the book of Isaiah 60:22, "**A little one shall become a thousand, and a small one a strong nation, I, the Lord, will hasten it in its time.**" You and I are a Holy Nation according to the book of 1 Peter 2:10. This is what grace does; it turns a man into a nation. Inside you and I are a lineage of kings and queens, Amen. Never ever underestimate the power of Grace in your life.

Remain ever blessed.

Abrahamic Covenant of Grace Part 2

Genesis 12:2

"And I will bless you [with abundant increase of favours], and you will be a blessing [dispensing good to others]."

In the society we live in today, the words "bless you" have now been downgraded and are only used when someone sneezes. The words "bless you" have lost their significance. What does *bless* mean? Bless means to be empowered, so if I sneeze and someone says, "bless you" and I say "thank you", it means I have received the empowerment to keep on sneezing!

To be blessed means to be empowered to do something and remember, grace is God's ability given to you to accomplish something you cannot do with your own ability. Abraham was not blessed but when grace showed up, we see the blessing at work in Abraham's life. I am not talking about spiritual blessings, I talking about material blessings. In Genesis 13:1-5, the Bible says, **"So Abram left Egypt and travelled north into the Negev, along with his wife and Lot and all that they owned. (Abram was very rich in livestock, silver, and gold.) From the Negev, they continued travelling by stages toward Bethel, and they pitched their tents between Bethel and Ai, where they had camped before. This was the same place where Abram had built the altar, and there he worshiped the LORD again. Lot, who was travelling with Abram, had also become very wealthy with flocks of sheep and** goats, herds of cattle, and many tents. **But the land could not support both Abram and Lot with all their flocks and herds living so close together. So disputes broke out between the herdsmen of Abram and Lot. (At that time Canaanites and Perizzites were also living in the land.)"**

Can you see the blessing at work? Abraham became very rich in silver and in gold simply because God said, "I will bless you." The blessing was so much that it overflowed into the life of Lot. Brethren, when the Abrahamic covenant of Grace is at work in your life, not only will you be empowered, but you will also be a channel of empowerment to others. The Abrahamic covenant of Grace includes favour. God said, " I WILL BLESS YOU WITH ABUNDANT INCREASE OF FAVOUR" and you and I know that the favour of God is not something we work for to earn, but it is given. Please take note, when God says, "I WILL" He is saying to you and I that that is His will or desire for us. It is God's desire to favour you. This means that things just work with speed and at ease; you do not need to work for it. God is simply saying, "I will favour you so much; people around you will be blessed."

Joseph is an example of this. The Bible says concerning him in Genesis 39:2-3, **"The Lord was with Joseph, and he [though a slave] was a successful and prosperous man; and he was in the house of his master the Egyptian. And his master saw that the Lord was with him and that the Lord made all that he did to flourish and succeed in his hand."** Though Joseph was a slave, because the Lord's favour was upon him, he was a successful man. This means that it's not your job that makes you a successful man; it's the Abrahamic covenant of abundant increase of favour that makes you rich. Joseph was a rich slave because the Lord was with him. The grace of God can make you rich in any occupation. I am not saying you shouldn't aim to get a decent job, what I am saying is that it's not your job that makes rich, it's the blessing of the Lord.

Finally, in Acts 3:25-26, the Bible gives us a revelation of what Christ did for us. The Bible says concerning Jesus, **"It is you who are the sons of the prophets and of the covenant which God made with your fathers, saying to Abraham, 'AND IN YOUR SEED ALL THE FAMILIES OF THE EARTH SHALL BE BLESSED.' For you first, God raised up His Servant and sent Him to bless you by turning every one of you from your wicked ways."**

Brethren, isn't it exciting that God sent Jesus to bless you? Jesus was sent to us for one specific reason, TO BLESS (EMPOWER) US. As new believers in Christ, who are Spirit filled with the Almighty God living in us, we have the empowerment to dispense good to the entire earth. PRAISE GOD! Jesus was sent to empower you. This will really bless you if you pay attention to what I am about to write. Luke 10:19, **"Behold, I have given you authority to tread on serpents and scorpions, and over all the power of the enemy, and nothing will injure you."** Why? Because Jesus was sent to empower you to tread upon the enemy, PRAISE GOD.

Let Your Tithe be Watered With Words

Deuteronomy 26:1-3

"**And it shall be, when you come into the land which the Lord your God is giving you as an inheritance, and you possess it and dwell in it, that you shall take some of the first of all the produce of the ground, which you shall bring from your land that the Lord your God is giving you, and put it in a basket and go to the place where the Lord your God chooses to make His name abide. And you shall go to the one who is priest in those days, and say to him....**"

Did you know that tithing goes beyond giving God your ten percent? Many people tithe without understanding what tithing is, and others tithe and never say anything before putting it in the basket and taking it to their appointed place of worship.

Did you see what the scripture above said? God doesn't want you to just take your tithe and put it in the basket. No, if you do so, change your thinking. Now look at this. Hebrews 6:19 says, **"Jesus, having become High Priest forever according to the order of Melchizedek."** Under the new covenant we have with God, Jesus is our High Priest. The duty of the High Priest is to take the tithe and present it to God. Hebrews 7:8 says, **"Here mortal men receive tithes, but there He receives them, of whom it is witnessed that He lives."** When you tithe, take your money to Jesus the High Priest and say, "Thank you, for I am blessed." You must water your tithe with your words. Do not tithe casually, no, tithe rejoicing and speaking the word to that seed.

Remain ever blessed.

Receive God's Love

Ephesians 2:4-5

"But God, who is rich in mercy, because of His great love with which He loved us, even when we were dead in trespasses, made us alive together with Christ."

Ephesians 3:19

"... and to know the love of Christ, which surpasses knowledge, that ye might be filled with all the fullness of God."

The scriptures show us that God loves us. God loves us regardless of our state. Paul the apostle wrote to the church in Rome and said, "**Who shall separate us from the love of Christ?** *Shall* **tribulation, or distress, or persecution, or famine, or nakedness, or peril, or sword? As it is written: 'For Your sake we are killed all day long; we are accounted as sheep for the slaughter.' Yet in all these things we are more than conquerors through Him who loved us. For I am persuaded that neither death nor life, nor angels nor principalities nor powers, nor things present nor things to come, nor height nor depth, nor any other created thing, shall be able to separate us from the love of God which is in Christ Jesus our Lord.**"

Paul the apostle was fully convinced that no matter what he faced, God's love for him will never change. God hasn't changed yet. His love is from everlasting to everlasting and God wants you and me to receive His love.

People do not get along with themselves and with others for many reasons and one of them is self-hatred. The Bible teaches us to deny ourselves (Matthew 16:24) but the Bible never tells us to deny ourselves of the love that comes from God. As a matter of fact, Paul says in 1 Corinthians 12:31 to covet spiritual gifts. Once you seek that love that comes from God and rest in it, then you can learn to love yourself and others. The love of God will transform you from the inside, and as a result of the inward changes, there will be changes seen on the outside.

Change starts with you. "WHAT? I thought change starts with God?" No, change starts with you. Let me explain further. God loves us all. However, He never forces us to receive that love; He simply gives us a choice. Salvation is a gift but you have a choice whether to receive it or not. Deuteronomy 30:19 says, **"Today I have given you the choice between life and death, between blessings and curses. Now I call on heaven and earth to witness the choice you make. Oh, that you would choose life, so that you and your descendants might live."**

God is saying, *you decide. Choose to receive me and you will be blessed, if you reject me then you be cursed, the choice is yours.* Every change starts with you. Jesus said in Matthew 22:37-40, **"You shall love the LORD your God with all your heart, with all your soul, and with all your mind. This is *the* first and greatest commandment. And *the* second *is* like it: 'You shall love your neighbour as yourself.' On these two commandments hang all the Law and the Prophets."** If you want better relationships, you must love the Lord, yourself and others. You cannot give what you do not have. If you do not have love for yourself, you cannot love others no matter how much you wish to love them. This kind of love, my friend, comes from God. Once you learn to love yourself, it makes it easier for you to love others. If you see someone lacking money, because you love yourself and cannot imagine yourself in that situation, you give to the other person. I hope this helps.

One final thing I will add: many know that God loves them but do not believe it. It's not enough to know God loves you, you must believe it. John the apostle said in 1 John 4:15, **"So we have come to know and to believe the love that God has for us."** It is in believing that God loves you that you experience true inner change.

Understand Your Uniqueness and Who You Are in Christ

To get along with others, you must and I mean *you must* understand who you are in Christ. In finding out your uniqueness, you know the area you stand out from others. For instance, there can be two faith preachers. One preaches on how to get faith and the other on how to develop your faith. The truth is they both preach on faith but their messages are different. What am I trying to say? You are different from others. You may attend the same church, or live in the same home, but you're different.

To discover your difference, fellowship with God. One mistake people make is to try to be like somebody else. DO NOT try to be like anybody else, but receive God's love for you and be confident in yourself. Love others, and appreciate them but you must first learn to appreciate who God has made you. Your gift may not be as big as others', but that gift God has given you is important. If you do not know what your gifts and talents are, just spend time with God, volunteer at your church, and by doing the things of God, your gifts will be discovered. I discovered my gift to write simply by just writing any revelation I have. I discovered my gift to preach the word because I spent time with God and His word, started preaching to myself, and served in my Christian union and university. Through serving, my gift was refined.

Learn to love yourself and appreciate yourself, because when you do so, you become more effective and as a result of this, you learn to love and appreciate others even if they don't appreciate you.

Whose Report Do You Believe?

Isaiah 53:1

"Who has believed our report?"

Do you believe the report of the doctor that says that you are sick or the report of Jesus that says you are healed? Matthew 8:17, **"This fulfilled the word of the Lord through the prophet Isaiah, who said, 'He took our sicknesses and removed our diseases.'"**

Do you believe the report that says that there is no job and there is scarcity or the report that says, **"in the time of famine you shall have more than enough."** (Psalm 37:19)

Do you believe in the report that says that there is no hope for your children, or the report that says, **"The seed of upright shall be mighty upon the earth?"** (Psalm 112:1-2).

Do you believe the report that says that you are barren or the report that says, **"none shall be barren in the land. There shall nothing cast their young, nor be barren, in thy land: the number of thy days I will fulfil."** (Exodus 23:6)

Do you believe in the report that says there is no hope for you or the report that says there is hope in the future? **"'So there is hope for your future,' declares the LORD."** (Jeremiah 31:17)

105

As a young person, do you believe you can break free of that addiction? **"He will call upon me, and I will answer him; I will be with him in trouble, I will deliver him and honour him."** (Psalm 91:15)

Do you believe what the media says or what the word says? **"But his delight is in the law of the LORD, and on his law he meditates day and night."** (Psalm 1:2)

Do you believe that that wayward child cannot serve the Lord or do you believe the word of the Lord that says, **"All your sons will be taught by the LORD, and great will be your children's peace**." (Isaiah 54:13)

Do you believe your child can never regain his voice back or do you believe the word that says there is nothing too hard for God? **"Jesus looked at them and said, 'With man this is impossible, but with God all things are possible.'"** (Matthew 19:26)

Do you believe in the report that says VICTORY?

Let me ask you again, whose report do you believe?

You are God's Masterpiece; The Apple of His Eye

Ephesians 2:10

¹⁰ For we are God's masterpiece. He has created us anew in Christ Jesus, so we can do the good things he planned for us long ago. (NLT)

A lot of people walk around looking sad because they feel that they are not beautiful enough to fit into a specific group. People condemn themselves all the time calling themselves names, mentioning how fat they are, or how skinny they look. They let people's words affect how they feel concerning themselves, but I'm telling you that you are beautiful just the way you are.

When the Creator made you in the beginning, He looked at you and said, "This is good." Genesis 1:31 tells us that God looked at all He had made and said, "This is good." This means God loves you and thinks you are good enough. People will say mean things to you and call you names. People will make fun of you because of your height, your shape, or your size, but do not let that get to you. Let God's word concerning you give you comfort.

I am not encouraging you to eat a lot and do nothing, but what I'm telling you is that you are beautiful, and if you're a guy, you are handsome and God loves you. I would encourage you to stay fit and exercise because that is good for you.

People will tell you that you are ugly and that you are not good enough. People will scoff at you and cause you to doubt if someone will marry a person like you. No, don't listen to that because your Boaz and Ruth are on their way. Do not let the media determine how you should look.

Do not let people decide your emotions and feelings, let God's word be your addiction.

You should wake up every morning and look into the mirror and say to yourself, "I am beautiful the way God made me, I am handsome, I am God's prized possession and I am the apple of his eye. I bring God joy and glory, my spouse is on the way." Your mind will tell you the opposite but you must speak the positive. The scripture tells us in Proverbs 18:21 that life and death are in the power of the tongue. The words you speak to yourself are life boomerangs. They will bring back what you say. Speak God's word to yourself. Let God's word determine your beauty.

You are beautiful and I will say this again: you are beautiful!

Please feel free to send this to other people you know who feel defeated or sceptical about their looks. Let them know how God sees them. Let them know that they are the apple of God's eye and that is why He sent Jesus to die for them so that He can restore them and beautify their lives.

You Are Worth It

Ephesians 3:8

"Though I am the least deserving of all, He graciously gave me the privilege."

Many times, because of our past errors, we shy away from God's unlimited grace. Some of us have been battling with addictions such as pornography, smoking, etc. but because we lack knowledge of God's mercy and lack faith in trusting God to help us, we run away from Him. No matter how much you have missed the mark on your journey of Christianity, God is calling you to come back and receive His mercy. God's word says in Hebrews 4:6, **"Let us then approach the throne of grace with confidence, so that we may receive mercy and find grace to help us in our time of need."** To come boldly means to approach God with confidence knowing that He will receive you back. David said in Psalm 51:11, **"Cast me not away from thy presence,"** and Jesus said in John 6:37, **"Whoever comes to me I will never drive away."**

You might not be a Christian but you're reading this. No matter your error, or what you are struggling to break free of e.g. pornography or smoking, Jesus says, "Come unto me and you shall find rest unto thy soul." Your soul, your being, is important to Christ. He can help you break free from your addictions if only you open up and trust in Him. No matter what you have done or how guilty you feel, God's grace and mercy are open for you to receive. Now, you might think *I haven't done anything, I'm ok, I don't need Jesus.* Well, see if any of these apply to you:

109

Ephesians 5: **"When you follow the desires of your sinful nature, the results are very clear: sexual immorality, impurity, lustful pleasures, idolatry, sorcery, hostility, quarrelling, jealousy, outbursts of anger, selfish ambition, dissension, division, envy, drunkenness, wild parties, and other sins like these. Let me tell you again, as I have before, that anyone living that sort of life will not inherit the Kingdom of God."**

Revelation 21:8 **"But cowards, unbelievers, the corrupt, murderers, the immoral, those who practice witchcraft, idol worshipers, and all liars—their fate is in the fiery lake of burning sulphur. This is the second death."**

The scriptures above are not meant to scare you, but to reshape your mind and help you see yourself. The apostle Paul was a sinner, but he encountered God's mercy and now he has eternal life with Jesus. You too can receive eternal life by calling out to Jesus and following His will for your life.

Amen. You are loved and worth it, so receive God's mercy now.

God can turn your life around, from a sinner to a winner. Paul was a sinner but is now a winner in the gospel of Jesus.

Your Best Days Are Still Ahead

J ob 8:8

"And though your beginning was small, your latter days will be very great."

Do not despise the season you are in right now because the seeds you sow today will be harvested tomorrow. Though the season you are in does not look like where you want to be, remember this: it is only a stepping stone and not the end. Paul said to Timothy in 1 Timothy 4:12, **"Don't let anyone think less of you because you are young."** Right now you might look small, people might ridicule you and say you amount to nothing but I want to tell you today that you have a great future ahead of you. People's opinion about you is only facts but not the truth. Do not ridicule where you are now because where you are now could be part of God's plan for where you need to be and if you are in the wrong place, God will direct you to where you need to be. All you need to do is to take heed and follow His leadings.

Also, do not settle for where you are now, but look forward to greater days. The greatest enemy to tomorrow's success is yesterday's accomplishment. Be determined to move forward regardless of people's opinions. The scripture above is good, but to see better day, you need to be determined to move forward. Abraham is a perfect example. The scripture tells us in Romans 4:18 and 20: **"Even when there was no reason for hope, Abraham kept hoping— believing that he would become the father of many nations. For God had said to him, 'That's how many descendants you will have.' Yet he did not waver**

111

through unbelief regarding the promise of God, but was strengthened in his faith and gave glory to God, being fully persuaded that God had power to do what he had promised." This means that though Abraham looked fatherless he still hoped for better days. He still believed that the future he saw would come to pass.

Friend, you have better days ahead of you. I challenge you to look beyond where you are now and look ahead of you. I see your latter days being like the latter end of Job's and even greater.

Job 42:10 **"The LORD blessed the latter part of Job's life more than the former part."**

The tide is changing for you.

Love, The Power to Transform Part 1

1 Corinthians 13:7

"Love bears up under anything and everything that comes, and is ever ready to BELIEVE THE BEST OF EVERY PERSON."

Love is the greatest force that exists. The love of God in our hearts knows no barriers because it is alive and powerful, it is sharper than the sharpest two-edged sword, cutting between soul and spirit, between joint and marrow. It exposes our innermost thoughts and desires. This means the love of God that flows through us is able to penetrate into the spirit of others. It can cut into them and expose our thoughts and desires for them. The love of God in our hearts has the power to invest the best of us into others that God has put in our care and those outside of the faith. The love of God is a transformable love when invested into people around us. A great man said, "Nobody cares what you know, until they know that you care."

When you choose to believe the best in others, or when you go the extra mile to ensure that the other person succeeds, you are being like your heavenly father. Love is what compels you to believe in that friend, your spouse, your children and other loved ones. The same scripture says, "Love never gives up." This means that if you really love the person and the people you interact with, you will never give up on them. Love is a transformable force. If you continue to love and remain committed, you allow God to work freely through you even though you may not see and understand the end result.

113

No matter what the situation might be, no matter how that co-worker, friend, child might behave, just love them tirelessly. Jesus said in Luke 6:35, **"Give expecting nothing in return."** This means love continually.

Three things will last forever: faith, hope, and love- and the greatest of these is LOVE.

Love, The Power to Transform Part 2

Luke 6:35

"But love...... and be kind and good (doing favours so that someone derives benefit from them.)"

Jesus gave a specific command, to love. The world operates by the "ME FIRST SYSTEM" but this is not so in the kingdom of God. God does not oppose your looking after yourself but what he does oppose is self-centeredness. What God really wants is for His children to love and care for others.

The love that transforms is the love that cares for others. If you have tension with somebody, choose to love that person. That person could be the one God has appointed to serve some of your needs. God did not say *if you feel like it, love* he said *make love a practice.* This means to have consistent, fervent love for anybody who mistreats you and for those that are close to you. The God kind of love prays for somebody that mistreats them and invokes God's favour upon their life.

Everybody needs to feel loved and accepted. Your co-worker, roommate, or even spouse might have a reason to why they behave as they do, and as a child of God your duty is to love them, and pray for them, even if they mistreat you and the more you sow that love, the more that person will begin to change. Love that person even if they do not deserve it because the truth is that none of us deserve the love of God.

When you love that unlovable person, you are heaping burning coals of shame upon that person (Romans 12:20) and you are acting like your father in heaven who does good to the ungrateful and the wicked. In other words, they become convicted by the goodness of God through you to the point they freely repent and give themselves to Jesus Christ as Lord and Saviour. The book of Luke 17:1-10 tells us about a man called Zacchaesus who was a notorious sinner. Jesus met with him and loved him to the point where Zacchaesus was convicted by God's love and said '' **will give half my wealth to the poor, Lord, and if I have cheated people on their taxes, I will give them back four times as much!''** [9] **Jesus responded, "Salvation has come to this home today, for this man has shown himself to be a true son of Abraham.** [10] **For the Son of Man came to seek and save those who are lost''.** God's love does not condemn, it convicts. This means as you love the unlovable people, your love for that person will convict such person and change their life.

Prepare For Your Harvest

L uke 8:5

"A farmer went out to sow his seed"

Proverbs 24:27, **"Prepare your work outside, and get your fields ready. Afterwards, build your house."**

Two farmers were expecting rain from God. One of them whilst waiting for rain went out to prepare his field, whilst the other was waiting for perfect conditions. Which one of them do you think God will give rain to?

The first one, of course. God will give the first one rain simply because he expressed his faith by putting it to action. The scripture tells us in Hebrews 11:1, **"Faith is the confidence that what we hope for will actually happen; it gives us assurance about things we cannot see."** The farmer who went out to sow had the faith that the rain he hoped for would actually happen even though he hasn't seen it. That is faith at work. Do not wait for perfect conditions before you start preparing.

Ecclesiastes 11:1 says, **"Cast your bread upon the water,"** and Ephesians 5:26 helps us to see that water is the word of God. Cast your seed, into what God says, and you will find it. Ecclesiastes 11:4 also says Farmers who wait for perfect weather never plant. If they watch every cloud, they never harvest. This means if you wait till things get better before you start preparing, you may end up waiting for a long time. Do not wait for perfect conditions.

117

So are you expecting a child from God? Go out and buy baby clothes, and toys for yourself and others who are expecting miracle children. You want money? Sow money. You want a friend? Be a friend. You want a car? Do your driving lessons. You want to start a business? Have a business plan. Whatever God has laid in your heart, go out and prepare your field. Do not wait for perfect conditions. Further down, verse 6 says, **"In the morning sow your seed, and in the evening do not withhold your hand; for you do not know which will prosper, either this or that, or whether both alike will be good."**

I highlighted those two just for emphasis sake. Sow your seed; do not withhold your hand. This means don't be stingy with what you have, sow it and do not withhold it. Remember Proverbs 11:24, **"One person gives freely, yet gains even more; another withholds unduly, but comes to poverty."** The farmer that did nothing was withholding his seed and that is why God will not give him rain. Don't let tough times be your excuse for withholding. The church in 2 Corinthians 8 was in deep poverty, yet they sowed into the ministry with joy. Do not let the absence of money keep you from sowing your talents. Do not focus on what you lack, but focus on what you have and invest that into the kingdom of God. Please be an addict to sowing.

You are a farmer in this kingdom, therefore sow and do not withhold your seed. Do not wait for perfect conditions. Remember, James 1:22-25, **"But be doers of the word, and not hearers only, deceiving yourselves. For if anyone is a hearer of the word and not a doer, he is like a man observing his natural face in a mirror; for he observes himself, goes away, and immediately forgets what kind of man he was. But he who looks into the perfect law of liberty and continues in it, and is not a forgetful hearer**

but a doer of the work, this one will be blessed in what he does."

In conclusion: sow your seed, prepare your field, and that thing that you are expecting from God will actually happen.

Receive Your Inheritance

Ephesians 1:11
"In Him we have obtained an inheritance."

The cross and the death of Jesus have made available everything you need. When Jesus died, He didn't just take away your sins, that was just a part of it. Jesus died to restore THE BLESSINGS Adam lost in Genesis.

Through the blood of Jesus, you have access to everything in God's will. God's will is for you to prosper in all things and be in good health. 3 John 2 says, **"Dear friend, I hope all is well with you and that you are as healthy in body as you are strong in spirit."** Through the blood of Jesus, you have an inheritance. You have an inheritance of favour, business, education, marriage, children with your name written on it.

You no longer have to live in lack and want. Stop begging God because through Christ's death, everything God has belongs to you. Galatians 3:29 tells us that now that we belong to Christ, we are the true children of Abraham. We are his heirs and all God's promised to Abraham belongs to us.

This is a quote from the Believer's Voice of Victory magazine by Kenneth and Gloria Copeland and I believe it will enlighten your understanding on this subject:

"Diana was asleep when Richard returned from the meeting. However, she roused him and urged him to read the book *Believers Authority* by Kenneth Hagin. Richard stayed up most of the night reading. Afterwards he knelt to pray and their 3 -year- old daughter curled up on the floor beside him and slept.

Lord, Richard prayed, I am learning from brother Hagin that it is your will for us to be healed and walk in health. I'm confused. I've been taught that sometimes it is not Your will.

'Behold your daughter,' God said, 'do you love her?'

Richard: More than life itself

God: Do you want her sick?

Richard: No, I'd rather take it myself

God: Do you want her hungry?

Richard: No

God: Do you want her poor?

Richard: No

God: I also love my children and I never want to see them hungry, sick or poor."

Friend, wake up to the reality of your inheritance in Christ. You never have to be sick or live in poverty. God took your sickness and poverty upon Himself so that you don't have to experience it. You have an inheritance in Christ, receive it by faith.

Dealing With Reproach From Men

1 Timothy 4:10

"For therefore we both labour and suffer reproach, because we trust in the living God, who is the Saviour of all men, specially of those that believe."

Have you ever felt like giving up your faith because people mock you about trusting in Jesus? If so, take strength from this and know that you are not alone.

One of the things we go through as believers is mockery and persecution because of our faith in Christ. Mockery may not be a result of the bad things you have done in the past, mockery could come simply because of your faith in Christ. Persecution may not be as big as what the apostles went through or people in the third world countries, it could be people taunting you at work or your friends or family making fun of you. However, no matter the reproach you face, there is a key to overcoming it and I will show you from the scriptures.

There was a man called Job in the Bible. According to the book of Job chapter 1, this man was a wealthy man and the greatest man in the east during his time. Furthermore in that scripture, we see that Job lost all he had by the reason of the devil striking him with sickness. In the midst of Job's challenges, the dearest person to him, his wife, said in Job 2:9, **"Are you still maintaining your integrity? Curse God and die."** This shows that the people that can mock you the most are those living in the same home as you. In Genesis 37, we are told about this young man called Joseph. At the

122

age of 17, Joseph had a dream that he would one day become a ruler. The same scripture tells us that his brothers hated him and were jealous of him because of his dream. One day, Jacob, Joseph's father, sent him to see to his brothers' welfare. When his brothers saw him coming from afar, they said amongst themselves, "Here comes the dreamer."

David the psalmist said in Psalm 42:9-11, "I say to God my Rock, 'Why have you forgotten me? Why must I go about mourning, oppressed by the enemy?' My bones suffer mortal agony as my foes taunt me, saying to me all day long, 'Where is your God?' Why, my soul, are you downcast? Why so disturbed within me? Put your hope in God, for I will yet praise Him, my Saviour and my God."

The enemy has a way of oppressing God's people but in the midst of oppression, David said, "Put your hope in God and praise Him." Jesus confirms this in Matthew 5:10-11 "Blessed are those who are persecuted for righteousness' sake, for theirs is the kingdom of heaven. Blessed are you when they revile and persecute you, and say all kinds of evil against you falsely for My sake. Rejoice and be exceedingly glad, for great is your reward in heaven, for so they persecuted the prophets who were before you."

No matter the reproach you are facing because of your faith in Christ, no matter how much people taunt you, see that as an opportunity to rejoice in the Lord. Remember, the Bible teaches in Galatians 3:26, **"For you are all children of God through faith in Christ Jesus."**

Some reading this might be taunted by family members because they do not have the fruit of the womb. Rejoice in the Lord.

123

Finally, God said in Isaiah 49:23, **"Kings and queens will serve you and care for all your needs. They will bow to the earth before you and lick the dust from your feet. Then you will know that I am the LORD. Those who trust in me will never be put to shame."** What does this mean? Those who mock you will end up serving you. Do not hate those who mock you, but love them and do good to them as Jesus commanded. By loving them and praying for them and doing good to them you will heap burning coals on their heads, and the LORD will reward you. (Proverbs 25:21)

Remain ever blessed.

Run With Endurance

Hebrews 12:1

"Therefore, since we are surrounded by such a huge crowd of witnesses to the life of faith, let us strip off every weight that slows us down, especially the sin that so easily trips us up, and let us run with endurance the race God has set before us."

God has a place for you in this life. Your birth on this earth was not by accident; God put you here with a purpose. There is a race set before you. This race is your future and the prize God has set before you at the end of your race in life. The race God has put before you is what will bring you fulfilment, give you a sense of purpose and most importantly bring God the glory. You have a future ahead of you, so you have to run with endurance. The Free Dictionary defines endurance as: "the act, quality, or power of withstanding hardship or stress." This means we must run with firmness, and persistence, regardless of difficulties.

Children of God, we all face challenges but challenges should give us the opportunity to persist without given up. James chapter 1:2-3 says, **"Dear brothers and sisters, when troubles come your way, consider it as an opportunity for great joy. For you know when your faith is tested, your endurance will grow."** To run this race effectively your faith must be tested, and when your faith is tested, your persistence, and firmness to withstand hardship will grow.

Notice that Hebrew 12:1 also tells us to get rid of every weight and sin. Weight and sin could be the small things you consider as nothing such as friends that pull you down, bad habits, pornography and other sins mentioned in the Bible. These are the weights that slow you down from achieving what God has for you. To enjoy God's best we have to obey what this scripture says.

I challenge you today to run with endurance. Have God's goal before you. Have something to look forward to. Oppositions will come but challenges notwithstanding, you will be an overcomer in the name of Jesus.

Serving God Pays

Job 36:11

"If they obey and serve Him, they shall spend their days in prosperity, and their years in pleasures."

Let me ask you this question, as a Christian, born again child of God, what are you doing with your life? Are you living life for yourself and for acquiring much for yourself? Or are you living for Jesus?

Many people, including so called born again Christians, are running this race of life for themselves, trying to attain heights by all means without serving Jesus. People want to be great without serving. People are going to the wrong places to find fulfilment of their destinies but the truth is this: anything achieved outside of God amounts to zero no matter your effort. Matthew 16:24 says, **"Then Jesus said to His disciples, "If anyone would come after me, he must deny himself."** This simply means you must give up your own passions to follow Him. Following God costs, but it also pays. Peter said in Mark 10:28 **"We have left everything to follow you, 'I tell you the truth,' Jesus replied, 'no one who has left home or brothers or sisters or mother or father or children or fields for me and the gospel will fail to receive a hundred times as much in this present age (homes, brothers, sisters, mothers, children and fields—and with them, persecutions) and in the age to come, eternal life.'"**

To follow God, you must deny yourself completely and give yourself entirely to His will. Look at the promises God made

127

in Job 36:11 combined with Mark 10:28-30. When serving God you are not losing out, but when serving yourself, you will end up in frustration. Choose to serve the Lord today and you shall live your days in prosperity and years in pleasure. Jesus said that they who serve Him will be honoured and by serving God, years will be added to your life (Proverbs 3:2).

Speaking Words of Faith to the Mountain

Mark 11:23-24

"And Jesus answering saith unto them, 'Have faith in God. For verily I say unto you, that whosoever shall say unto this mountain, "Be thou removed, and be thou cast into the sea" and shall not doubt in his heart, but shall believe that those things which he saith shall come to pass; he shall have whatsoever he saith.'"

This scripture, I believe, is very significant because it teaches they key of defeating any situation. What is this key you ask? Words. A lot of times, many people magnify their situations instead of speaking to the situation. We examine the situation, and explain the situation. Don't get me wrong, there is nothing wrong in telling people what you are going through, but there is a problem if that is all you do. Before Jesus said these words, let's take a look at what had happened previously.

"So Jesus came to Jerusalem and went into the Temple. After looking around carefully at everything, He left because it was late in the afternoon. Then He returned to Bethany with the twelve disciples. The next morning as they were leaving Bethany, Jesus was hungry. He noticed a fig tree in full leaf a little way off, so He went over to see if He could find any figs. But there were only leaves because it was too early in the season for fruit. Then Jesus said to the tree, 'May no one ever eat your fruit again!' And the disciples heard Him say it."

129

Jesus was faced with a situation in that scripture. He was hungry and the fig tree wasn't producing any fruit. Notice Jesus didn't explain why the fig tree wasn't producing, HE SPOKE TO IT.

After that, Jesus now said to us, **"Verily I say unto you, that whosoever shall say unto this mountain."** It's time we stop explaining our mountains and started speaking to the mountains. Say, "Mountain of sickness I say be cast out IN JESUS' NAME. Mountain of stagnation I say be cast out." Speak to your mountains.

Joshua 1:8 says, **"This Book of the Law shall not depart from your mouth."** Do not just speak words, but speak the word of God to the situation. Tell that situation what the word of the Lord says. Jesus said, **"The words that I speak to you, they are spirit and they are life."** The word of God brings life to everything. Speak life into your home, children, finances, career, health and all that concerns you. Do not be moved by what you see; be moved by what God says. If you are single, and you feel like there's no one out there for you, say to that situation, "I am married in Jesus' name." If you have a terminal disease, say, "He Himself took my infirmities and bore my sickness and by Jesus' stripes I am healed." (Matthew 8:17, Isaiah 53:5) this means that if Jesus took it, it has no right in your body.

You may not have much finance and you're believing God for a breakthrough, say to your finances like the Psalmist said in Psalm 23:1, **"I shall not want**." Whatever the situation may be, speak the word of life into it say to that mountain, "Be removed." Do not talk yourself out of victory; talk your way into victory.

Notice, in Mark 11, when Jesus spoke to the tree, it didn't dry up immediately. The Bible says in verse 20, **"Now in the morning, as they passed by, they saw the fig tree dried**
130

up from the roots. And Peter, remembering, said to Him, 'Rabbi, look! The fig tree which You cursed has withered away.'"

Sometimes you might not get the results you want immediately, but keep speaking the word and soon the situation will dry up from the root and wither away. Your words are like boomerangs; whatever you say is what you will have.

Proverbs 18:21, **"Death and life are in the power of the tongue, And those who love it will eat its fruit."**

Proverbs 18:20, **"A man's stomach shall be satisfied with the fruit of his mouth; and with the increase of his lips shall he be filled."**

I give you this charge: choose carefully what you say.

Tell Somebody What God Has Done For You

Luke 8:39

"Now go back to your family and tell them what God has done for you."

It's about time you tell somebody about the goodness of God in your life. Tell somebody what God has done for you. Do not keep the goodness of God to yourself, but tell somebody how great God is.

If you look around you, you will see a lot of broken-hearted people who need a touch from God. God does things in our lives so that we can testify to others that He is good. If you see someone who is struggling from an addiction God took you out of; tell that person what the Lord did for you. If you see a student struggling with an exam; tell the person how God helped you. If you see your neighbour struggling to handle their kids or finding it difficult to take their kids to school, be a helping hand and tell the person how God helped you.

Do not hide the goodness of God. There are people who need to know what God has done for you. Share your testimony with a friend. You never know how helpful your story can be. Your testimony is like water, it cools the flames of life. Your testimonies can be a life changer. Proverbs 10:11 says, **"The words of the godly are a life giving fountain."** Verse 20 says, **"The words of the godly encourage many."** Your words, your testimonies can bring life to the dry fountains of others. Even if God gave you new pair of shoes, tell someone no matter how small it is.

There is somebody that needs your testimony. God wants to heal others through the goodness He has done in your life. If you keep your testimonies to yourself, you will be deprived of more.

I challenge you today, just like Jesus said, go and tell your family what God has done for you. Your family are not only those in your home, but your family are your fellow human beings who are created in God's image.

The Power of a Praying Friend

Job 42:10

"And the LORD turned the captivity of Job, when he prayed for his friends: also the LORD gave Job twice as much as he had before. "

I believe this scripture is a powerful one. There is power in praying for your friends. The greatest help you can give a friend is to show them love by your actions and also pray for them.

Standing in the gap for your friends is powerful because it:

Helps your relationships to grow stronger. In John 17:11, Jesus prayed for His disciples. He said, "Now protect them by the power of Your name so that they will be united just as we are." To be united means to be one with another, to grow as one and that is what prayer does. Prayer keeps friends united even though they are not in the same place.

Helps your friend in times of trouble. When you see your friend that you love in trouble, whether born again or not, go to the Lord in prayer and ask God to deliver him. Remind God of what His word says, tell Him He said in Psalm 91:15 "I will be with him in times of trouble, I will deliver him." Pray that God draw your unsaved friend to Himself. Call your friend, invite your friend to church and see what God will do.

If you have a friend you love and have had a quarrel with that person, do not hate the person, but pray that God will bless the person, and invoke God's blessing upon them as this is the teaching of Jesus in Matthew chapter 5:44. Every night or morning when you kneel down, pray for your friends.

The perfect example is Job. Job prayed for his friends and God turned back his captivity. When you pray for your friends, it nourishes both yourself and your friends. God restores you and makes changes in your life.

So I challenge you today to be a praying friend and I know God will minister to you in return.

He Gives the Childless Woman a Family

Psalm 113:9

"He gives the childless woman a family, making her a happy mother."

There are a lot of people today who are believing God for the fruit of the womb, but I am writing to tell you that God will give you that child if you trust in Him. This scripture gives us an assurance that God is a doer of His word.

Sarah, our covenant mother, could not give her husband Abraham a child. Sarah doubted even when the angel told her in Genesis 18:10 that she would have a son. She asked herself, "How could a worn out woman like me enjoy such pleasure, especially when my master-my husband- is also old?" But because God is so good, we are told in Genesis 21:1-2 that the Lord kept His word and did for Sarah exactly what He had promised: she became pregnant, and she gave birth to a son for Abraham.

God can do the same for you if you just believe. God will give you that child that you have been praying for. No matter the medical verdict, or how old you are, God is still able. I believe this message is meant for somebody reading it. If you are that person, begin to rejoice that God will make you a happy mother/ father and that He will give you a family of your own.

Confess this to yourself each morning and night:

- I am blessed with the fruit of the womb

136

- I am a mother/father of many generations
- I have my own family

Begin to see yourself in the light of God's word. In Romans 4:18-23 the scripture tells us that, **"Against all hope, Abraham in hope believed and so became the father of many nations, just as it had been said to him, 'So shall your offspring be.' Without weakening in his faith, he faced the fact that his body was as good as dead—since he was about a hundred years old—and that Sarah's womb was also dead. Yet he did not waver through unbelief regarding the promise of God, but was strengthened in his faith and gave glory to God, being fully persuaded that God had power to do what He had promised. This is why it was credited to him as righteousness."**

Start today by hoping even though your situation looks dead. Strengthen your faith according to God's word that He will make you happy and give you a family of your own. I see God giving you your own testimony. In less than 10 months, you will share your own testimony.

Please feel free to send this message to anybody you know that believes God for the fruit of the womb. I believe the power of Jesus can flow through the message of hope and I know that in 9 months' time, somebody will testify to the glory of the Lord.

How the Grace of God Manifests Itself

2 Corinthians 8:7

"I want you to excel also in this gracious act of giving."

Giving is part of the very nature of God. The scripture tells us in John 3:16, **"for God so loved the world that he GAVE His only begotten son"** and the scripture tells us in Matthew 20:28, **"Just as the Son of Man did not come to be served, but to serve, and to GIVE His life as a ransom for many."** Why was Jesus able to give up his life? The grace of God was upon Him. If we are the body of Christ, then that means the same grace that was upon Jesus is available to us too, if we tap into it.

The grace of God is what we need as believers because without the grace of God, our efforts amount to nothing. The reason why the early church was tremendously blessed is not because they could pray hard, or because they were just believers, that is part of it. The ultimate reason why they were so blessed and God could use them properly was because they had the very nature of God which was giving. The Bible says in 2 Corinthians 8:1-2, **"We want to tell you further, brethren, about the grace (the favour and spiritual blessing) of God which has been evident in the churches of Macedonia [arousing in them the desire to give alms] For in the midst of an ordeal of severe tribulation, their abundance of joy and their depth of poverty [together] have overflowed in wealth of lavish generosity on their part."**

138

These people were deeply poor, yet they were generous givers. You will agree with me that that can only be done by the grace of God, to give in poverty. This also tells me that hard times should not stop us from giving to God and fellow brethren.

People of God, when we look away from ourselves and cater for the needs of others, God will make sure that our needs are met. Jesus said in Luke 6:38, **"Give, and [gifts] will be given to you; good measure, pressed down, shaken together, and running over, will they pour into [the pouch formed by] the bosom [of your robe and used as a bag]. For with the measure you deal out [with the measure you use when you confer benefits on others], it will be measured back to you."**

Friend, you can never out give God. When you give generously, God promises that your return shall be greater.

I love these two verses because they inspire me to give. Acts 4:32 says, **"Now the company of believers was of one heart and soul, and not one of them claimed that anything which he possessed was [exclusively] his own, but everything they had was in common and for the use of all."**

Everything they had, they used it to serve others because they love God and their fellow brethren. If we as the body of Christ can follow that sort of grace, then God will bless us so much to the extent that this world will be a better place for Christ.

So I beseech you, brethren, to give liberally. I'm speaking in terms of material things. Anyone could easily give you their time, pray for you, and send you texts in difficult times and do not get me wrong that is good, but how many people can give out of their material things to benefit others or even God in hard times? The truth is only a few.

I hope you have been blessed by this. Remain forever blessed,

Ademola.

Growing in the Knowledge of God by His Word

2 Peter 3:18

"But grow in the grace and knowledge of our Lord and Saviour Jesus Christ. To him be glory both now and forever! Amen."

I got born again in January 2009 after attending a Bible study course at my previous local church, *Winners Chapel*, called *Word of Faith Bible Institute,* and ever since then, I desired to study the word of God. As the book of 1 Peter 2:2 says, "**Like new-born babies, long for the pure milk of the word, so that by it you may grow in respect to salvation.**" This means that as a newborn baby desires milk, we should also have the desire to study the word. This desire can only be given to us by the Holy Spirit as the scripture in Philippians 2:13 shows: "**For God is working in you, giving you the desire and the power to do what pleases Him.**" I had an intense desire to know the word of God and grow in the knowledge of God. I remember clearly, there were days I would spend up to 3-4 hours reading the Bible. The word of God all of a sudden became alive in my spirit man. The word of God was all I wanted to know. Nothing excited me more than to study the word of God. There were times I would watch TV with my family but after 30 minutes of television, I would quietly leave the sitting room to go and study the word of God. Church became a place I always wanted to be. I didn't mind spending the whole day at church. Brethren, the word can turn your life around if only you make the centre of your focus. The word of God took me to university, gave me confidence that I could make it through university, and the word gave me a job after university. The word of God gave me a better life, and gives me a hope and the assurance that my future is bright.

I have noticed one plague that is destroying this generation, especially young believers, and this is the fact that most people do not like reading. They can spend time watching nonsense programs on TV; they can go to church and never spend personal time in the word. Some read the word and do not understand it and don't even bother seeking more knowledge by reading other people's books, and because of IGNORANCE, the devil is devouring most people with his tricks. I heard a word from Bishop David Oyedepo. In one of his teachings he said, "READERS ARE LEADERS." I want to be a leader in my generation so I decided to start reading books. I will explain shortly why reading other people's books are vital in the Christian journey. Bishop David Oyedepo said, "The greatest enemy of destiny is ignorance." This lines up with what the word of God says in Hosea 4:6, **"My people are destroyed from lack of knowledge. Because you have rejected knowledge, I also reject you as my priests; because you have ignored the law of your God, I also will ignore your children."** Remember, we are to grow in knowledge, but sadly, this is not so in this generation as many lives are destroyed because they lack the knowledge of God's word.

The question is, how do I grow in knowledge of God?

Read anointed books.

Thank God for my previous church, Winners Chapel. One of the things I learnt from Winners as a young believer was to read books. The first time I entered the bookshop, it was like a spiritual buffet for me. I wanted to buy books so if a book

142

cost £8, I would save £2 a week until I was able to save enough to buy one book at the end of the month. Bishop Oyedepo's story inspired me. He said one day that he had been on a journey to America, and on his way back he had bought bags of books. When he got home, his wife thought it was clothes items he had bought, and when she opened the bag, she found books! I laughed and laughed but since my heart is into his ministry I imitated him. One day I went to the book store and spent between £80 to £100 on books. The shopkeeper asked me, "Why don't you save your money?" I told him to mind his own business. His life was a complete mess and I didn't want to be like him. He was deviating from the faith, and he wanted to take me along but I stood my ground against him.

Today, many people wonder how I know so much and I tell them it's because I have a personal relationship with Jesus Christ, I desire more revelation from His word and therefore, I read books. The truth is, no man can fully understand the Bible but there are anointed individuals whom God has placed in the body of Christ to write anointed books so you and I can be set free. Maybe there are many things bothering you and you need an answer. Well, it's in a book and all you need to do is locate it. I grew in my knowledge of God through reading authors such as Kenneth Copeland, Kenneth Hagin and Bishop David Oyedepo among many other authors. Through their books, I know that poverty is history in my life. Their teachings via the help of the Holy Spirit have broken the mediocre mentality in my life. There are things about you that will never change until you read someone else's book. Some of the things that you and I are going through have been conquered by other people, and their testimony is in their books. Daniel in the Holy Scriptures said in Daniel 9:2, **"In the first year of his reign, I, Daniel, understood from the books according to the word of the LORD to Jeremiah the prophet that the**

143

number of years for the desolation of Jerusalem would be 70." Daniel is simply saying that he got his understanding of what would happen to Jerusalem by reading what God had said to Jeremiah the prophet. There are certain things about you that are written in a book by prophets, pastors and teachers in the body of Christ. Locate them and read it. A lady in my previous church didn't have a job, and after service she read a book called *Satan Get Lost*, and in 3 days, she got a job. I read a book by Bishop David Oyedepo called *Understanding Financial Prosperity* and ever since I read the book, I have not known poverty even when I have zero pounds in my account. The book made me understand that I can never be poor if I put the principles to work that God has put in place such as tithing, sowing into your pastor's life, giving to your parents, giving to the poor and giving to the kingdom of God.

Moreover, reading books sharpens your mind. God speaks to me when I read books by Kenneth Copeland. I hear from Him clearly. Kenneth Copeland is my spiritual mentor because his testimonies relate to my personal life. Through his teachings, I rub minds with God easily and my understanding of God's word changes from one level to another.

Do not let ignorance destroy your life. You are not too young to read and hear from God. If you cannot read big books, start with small ones. Reading books helped me grow in my Christian journey and I want you to grow as well. Anyone that knows me knows that I can give books out easily because I have that desire to impact people with the word. You can pray from now till tomorrow, but some answers you will never get until you sit down and read. A student doesn't just study the text book to prepare for exams. If you do that, there's a 70% chance of failure. A good student who wants to pass will not only read his text books, he or she will read other people's notes, write their own notes and do some research online. As we graduate from university, our lecturers will fail us if we do not reference other people, even though the work they give us is from a single textbook. Likewise, you will fail miserably if you do not study other people's materials. You cannot understand the Bible on your own. God would not give others the ability to write books if they were not needed. May the Lord help our understanding in Jesus' name. Though I have mentioned the benefits of reading books, please be aware that not all books you read are good. There are some that can wreck your life. The word of God is the most important book to read but if you do desire to pick up a book, allow God to guide you into which book to buy.

God Believes the Best Of You

1 Corinthians 13:7

"Love is ever ready to believe the best of every person."

I want to ask you this question. Even though you know God loves you, do you feel that the people close to you, the people you live with, don't care and believe the best about you? If that is so, I want to tell you that God believes the best of you.

You ask, why? I know this because in His word He said in Jeremiah 29:11, **"'For I know the plans I have for you,' declares the LORD, 'plans to prosper you and not to harm you, plans to give you hope and a future.'"** God's thoughts of you are filled with hope and with love. God has your interests in mind. God believes the best in you even if nobody else does. Joseph had a dream from God, but his brothers didn't believe in his dreams. Instead, they despised him and mocked him. The people you live with might mock you, but have this in mind: God believes the best of you.

I want you to start dreaming big and filling your heart with hope again knowing that God believes the best in you. God is love and love is always ready to believe the best in you. The scripture tells us in Ephesians 3:20, **"Now to him who is able to do immeasurably more than all we ask or imagine, according to his power that is at work within us..."** God is able to bring out the best in you if only you trust in Him. God is love and His desire is for you to succeed in His plans.

Additional Resources to Supplement your Reading

You Are Not Alone

Hebrews 12:1

"Therefore, since we are surrounded by such a huge crowd of witnesses to the life of faith."

In this race of life, you are not alone. In everything we go through, we have witnesses, people who have been there before and can testify that God was faithful to see them through their issues and keeps His promises to them.

In the book of Genesis 37- 40, the Bible tells us about a young man called Joseph. Joseph was a young man who was filled with dreams and hopes. Joseph was so excited that he told his brothers, but his brothers hated him for this and mistreated him. Joseph's brothers sold him into slavery to the land of Egypt (Genesis 37:12). Joseph lived in a man named Potiphar's house. This man was Joseph's master.

Potiphar had a wife who lusted sexually after Joseph daily and constantly asked Joseph to lie with her. Joseph's response was, "How can I do this wickedness and sin against God?" (Genesis 39:9) Furthermore, the scripture tells us that he was sent to prison for the sin he did not commit (Genesis 39:20).

The scripture tells us that in all his troubles the Lord was with Joseph. Now, I am saying this to you: the Lord is with you. Genesis 39:2 says, "The Lord was with Joseph, and he was a successful man." In verse 21 of the same chapter after Joseph was thrown into prison, the scripture says that the Lord was with him. God works in mysterious ways. God

148

caused the prisoners to have dreams, and God gave Joseph the gift to interpret the dreams. God caused the king of Egypt to have a dream and nobody could interpret it except Joseph. I cannot tell you the full story but if you read Genesis 37-50, Joseph's life can testify that God is faithful. This story is too great to tell, I cannot write it all. God is too faithful.

Friend, no matter your mistreatment, no matter where life has taken you, no matter who mistreated you and judged you wrongly even though you did nothing wrong; you need to believe that the Lord is with you. These mistreatments happen but Romans 8:28 says, **"and we know that God causes everything to work together for the good of those who love God and are called according to his purpose for them."** I know that God will turn things around for your own good and when He does, remember to share your testimony about the Lord's doing in your life. Joseph's dream was to be a prime minister and God caused his mistreatment to work out for his good. Joseph said to his brothers in Genesis 50:20, **"You meant evil against me, but God meant it for good, in order to bring it about as it is this day, to save many lives."** That could be God's plan for your life. Your mistreatment can be God's pathway to your blessing. God can use your situation to bless not only you, but others including the ones who wronged you.

God is a faithful God.

God Has Your Best Interests at Heart

Isaiah 48:12

"Thus says the LORD, your Redeemer, the Holy One of Israel; I am the LORD your God who teaches you to profit, who leads you by the way that you should go."

A lot of people believe that God is depriving them from having a good life. People have been deceived into thinking that once they dedicate their life to God, they will live a life that is not fulfilling, without realising that God is the source of a truly fulfilling life. That is what Satan did to Adam and Eve. Satan deceived them into thinking that God was hiding something from them. He got them to question what God had said and to disobey Him. However, the Bible makes it clear that God has our best interests in His heart and that His thoughts toward us are good. For instance, the scriptures tell us in Jeremiah 29:11, **"For I know the thoughts I have toward you says the Lord, they are thoughts of good and not for evil, to give you a hope and a future."** If God's thoughts are good for me, then why is the world evil? The world is evil because the Bible tells us in 2 Corinthians 4:4, **"Satan, who is the god of this world, has blinded the minds of those who don't believe. They are unable to see the glorious light of the Good News. They don't understand this message about the glory of Christ, who is the exact likeness of God. "**

This makes it clear that Satan is the one behind the evil of this world. Jesus confirms this by saying in John 10:10, **"The thief comes only in order to steal and kill and destroy."**

Having showed us the one who is truly depriving us of God's best, Jesus also said concerning Himself, to show us that He has the best plan for us, in John 10:10, **"I came that they may have and enjoy life, and have it in abundance (to the full, till it overflows)."** *They* in this context are the ones who live for and trust in God for everything. God's desire for every human being is to have a fulfilled life if they will devote themselves to Him. The scriptures tell us in 2 Peter 3:9, **"Not desiring that any should perish, but that all should turn to repentance."** See what God said in Isaiah 48:17; He said, **"I am the one who teaches you which way to go and how to profit."** God wants you to enjoy this life. God said in Proverbs 3:2, **"My son, do not forget my teaching, but keep my commands in your heart, for they will prolong your life many years and bring you peace and prosperity."** God will give you peace and prosperity if only you devote yourself to Him.

Peter, before he became an apostle of Christ, was fishing but didn't catch anything. However, when he met with Jesus, Jesus said to him, "Cast thy net into the deep." Peter's response was, **'"Master, we have toiled all the night, and have taken nothing: nevertheless at thy word I will let down the net. And when they had this done, they inclosed a great multitude of fishes: and their net brake."** (Luke 5:5-6).

God's instruction is for our profit. Jesus told them what to do and their breakthrough happened. God said, **"If you diligently hearken to my voice, I will set thee high above all nations."** (Deuteronomy 28:1)

"All nations shall call you blessed." (Malachi 3:12)

Do not be deceived, God has a good plan for you. Your own part is to be obedient to Him, and even if you make mistakes, people mock you, or His instructions look stupid

151

to your natural senses, run back to God and allow Him to lead you.

God is Suddenly Turning Things Around

P salm 126:1

"When the LORD turned again the captivity of Zion, we were like them that dream."

Our God is a God of sudden changes. God is a specialist in making sudden changes in situations that seems impossible. In Exodus 3:7 the Lord said to Moses, **"I have surely seen the affliction of my people which are in Egypt, and have heard their cry by reason of their taskmasters; for I know their sorrows."** God knows your sorrows and He has heard your cries. God didn't stop at just knowing their sorrows, He said in verse 8, **"And I am come down to deliver them out of the hand of the Egyptians, and to bring them up out of that land unto a good land and a large, unto a land flowing with milk and honey."** God is coming down to change things for you in Jesus' name.

God is a specialist at making overnight changes. In Acts 16:25 the Bible says, **"At about midnight Paul and Silas were praying and singing hymns to God, and the other prisoners were listening to them. Suddenly there was such a violent earthquake that the foundations of the prison were shaken. At once all the prison doors flew open, and everyone's chains came loose."** Paul and Silas were singing and probably didn't know what would happen next, but the Bible says SUDDENLY. GOD IS MAKING A SUDDEN change in your life in JESUS' NAME, AND THAT CHANGE YOU WILL NOT RECOVER FROM. Suddenly there was an earthquake and their chains came loose. When God changes you, you are loosened from every captivity. When
153

God turned things around for Israel, He said that it was like a dream. Everything God does is amazing; it makes you wonder because God's acts are wonders.

When God changes your story, He will fill you with laughter. People will marvel and say, "Yes, indeed, God is real and He is with you." It will be like a dream. Get ready because God is making sudden change in your life. The Bible says in Luke 24:31, **"Then He stood up and rebuked the wind and waves, and suddenly all was calm."** This means that when God arises on your behalf, oppositions **suddenly** calm down. Matthew 26:75 "He went to her bedside the fever **suddenly** left, every sickness suddenly leaves when Jesus arises. Mark 1:31, **"You will grieve, but your grief will suddenly turn to wonderful joy when you see me again,"** when Jesus shows up, every breakdown turns to breakthrough.

Our God is an all of a sudden God so today; expect the sudden move of God. When Jesus shows up, **Suddenly** your anguish will turn to joy. **Suddenly** all is well, **Suddenly** you are healed! Suddenly you are promoted at work, **Suddenly** you are divinely connected, Suddenly your natural and spiritual eyes are opened! **Suddenly** He makes a way for you in wilderness, where there seems to be no way, **Suddenly** you will begin to have all around supernatural breakthroughs. When you have a relationship with Christ, **suddenly** you can become a new creation in Christ. **Suddenly** your sins are forgiven and **suddenly** errors are overlooked.

One last piece of encouragement. God said in Exodus 3:21, **"I will grant this people favour in the sight of the Egyptians; and it shall be that when you go, you will not go empty-handed"**

When God releases you from the oppositions, **SUDDENLY** all those who hate you will begin to favour you and give to you out of their own resources. There shall be wealth transfer when God makes a sudden change in your life.

God Makes Miracles Out of Our Mistakes

Romans 11:29
"For God's gifts and His call are irrevocable."

So many people are walking around with so much guilt in their hearts, feeling that God can never forgive them for all the wrong they have done. They think that God has abandoned them and changed His mind concerning them. No matter what you have done and how far you have gone, God can clean up your mess and turn it to a message. That is the reason He sent Jesus to die for you so that He can forgive you and make you new.

You might say, "But I have lied, stolen, and taken drugs, how can God forgive someone like me?" In Luke chapter 23:32-43, there were two thieves nailed next to Jesus at the cross. One of the thieves scoffed at Jesus but the other said to Jesus, "Remember me when you come into Your kingdom." And He (Jesus) said to him, "Truly I say to you, today you shall be with Me in Paradise." This means that Jesus received the thief in the last minute. We also have the story of the prodigal son in Luke chapter 15 who decided not to be with his father anymore and left his father's home to do what he desired. Soon afterwards, his life dried up and he thought to return to his father (God). The scripture tells us that his father saw him from afar and had compassion on him and welcomed him back home.

God can do the same for you. He will welcome you home if only you return and receive JESUS as your Lord and Saviour. It doesn't matter where you have been and what you have done, God still wants you back home. Go back to God and confess your sins. God will heal you and make miracles out of your mistakes.

God Will Generously Provide All You Need

2 Corinthians 9:8

"And God will generously provide all you need."

The God we serve is not a poor God; the God we serve is not a stingy God. The God we serve, our Father, is a generous God. God delights in giving you what he has. He has already made provision for all that you need and even much more than your mind can comprehend.

Never worry about your provision, all you need to do is seek God first in all that you do and live right in His sight, and then all your provisions shall be added to you. Your provisions are not limited to money alone. You have need of children, health, protection, marriage spouse, and so on. The majority of what is essential to living a good life is what money cannot buy. You need health to live and money cannot buy health. You need protection; otherwise you are fried chicken to the devil. You need favour, which money cannot buy. Money is needed, however, it is not all you need. You need peace, joy, love and most importantly, God Himself.

I want to share with you the insight God gave me in the story of Elijah and the widow of Zarephath. The main focus of that story is the widow and how God transformed her. However, I would like to shift the focus a bit. In 1 Kings 17:4-6, God commanded the ravens to feed Elijah, so the man was enjoying himself, but after a while, God caused the brook to dry up. Then God said to him in verse 9 "Arise, get thee to Zarephath, which belongeth to Zidon, and dwell there: behold, I have commanded a widow woman there to sustain thee."

What point am I trying to make? If you noticed, I highlighted the word *commanded* twice. The emphasis is that, no matter the dryness, God has commanded someone to bring the provision to you and if people don't yield, animals will. Psalm 37:18-19 assures us that day by day the Lord takes care of the innocent, and they will receive an inheritance that lasts forever. They will not be disgraced in hard times; even in famine they will have more than enough.

Believe and Have Faith in God For What You Ask

Mark 11:22, 24

"So Jesus turned, answered, and said to them 'have faith in God [constantly] for this reason I am telling you, whatever you ask for in prayer, believe [trust and be confident] that it is granted to you, and you will get it.'"

Most of us today, when we go to God, we go to him unsure if He will hear us. The scriptures tell us in 1 John 5:14-15, **"And this is the confidence (the assurance, the privilege of boldness) which we have in Him: [we are sure] that if we ask anything (make any request) according to His will (in agreement with His own plan), He listens to and hears us. And if (since) we [positively] know that He listens to us in whatever we ask, we also know [with settled and absolute knowledge] that we have [granted us as our present possessions] the requests made of Him."**

God is not interested in the amount of words that come out of our mouth, God is not interested how much we shout, or how long we pray, what God is really looking at is our faith. The question is, are you believing when you pray or are you just praying for the sake of it? Is your faith in your prayers?

As children of God, approach God in humility and boldness. Go to God believing based on His word. Let your prayers be rooted from God's word. Go to God knowing that He hears your prayers. Jesus said that when you believe, you shall have what you say. Notice that Jesus did not say, "When you cry you will receive", He did not say, "When you shout you will receive." Jesus said, "Believe that you have received what you asked for, then you shall have what you say." You get God's attention the moment you believe what He says in His word. God works in your direction when you believe even though what you ask for is not there. Believe God that you have received it, and then you will get it.

Remember that Hebrews 11:1-2 tells us that faith is the confidence that what we hope for will actually happen. It gives us assurance about things we cannot see. Your faith in God's word is what gives you the assurance that you've received what you ask for. Friend, faith is so important in prayer. Without faith, without believing that you have received, you cannot get it.

So I challenge you today to have faith in God.

Can All Your Worries Add a Moment to Your Life?

Matthew 6:27

"**Can all your worries add a single moment to your life? Of course not.**"

There are many issues that dominate your thoughts. These could be family issues, job related issues, or whatever it is that seems to dominate your thoughts. Jesus said, "Can all the worries you have add a moment to your life?"

People spend hours worrying about how to overcome their problems, but the truth is that worry never gets them anywhere. The moment you decide to carry the burden on yourself, you're doing yourself damage and you've taken the responsibility off God. I'm not implying that you shouldn't plan ahead or think about things, but do not let the things that bother you dominate your thoughts.

Jesus gave a practical truth of the damage worry does in people's lives in Matthew 13:22, "**As for what was sown among thorns, this is he who hears the Word, but the cares of the world and the pleasure and delight and glamour and deceitfulness of riches choke and suffocate the Word, and it yields no fruit.**"

Worry has the power to choke the truth of God in our hearts. God does not want you walking around with worry in your heart so He tells you to give all your burdens to Him (1 Peter 5:7).

162

Jesus gave us a simple example to follow. He said in Matthew 6:26, **"Look at the birds of the air; they do not sow or reap or store away in barns, and yet your heavenly Father feeds them. Are you not much more valuable than they? Can any one of you by worrying add a single hour to your life?"**

None of us have the capacity to carry all our burdens. People die unnecessarily because of stress. I pray that God will give you the grace to live a stress free life. The truth is, no matter how you worry about making ends meet, it cannot do you any good. Yes, plan and work hard, but let God give you the peace that surpasses all understanding. Live like the birds in the air and trust that your heavenly father will feed you. You are worth more to God than anything else.

Friend, I challenge you today to live a stress free life. Cast your burdens to the Lord because He cares so much for you. Trust in God to meet your needs this week. Jesus loves you, so cheer up.

Dream Big

Ephesians 3:20

"Now all glory to God, who is able, through His mighty power at work within us, to accomplish infinitely more than we might ask or think."

So many people have dreams trapped up inside of them. People are filled with potential that is waiting to manifest but their dreams have been put aside because they feel there is no hope or the people around them have talked them out of their dreams and told them it is impossible to achieve them. Parents are very good at that. Parents tell their kids to stop having that type of dream because it has never happened before and they believe their child does not have what it takes to accomplish that dream.

If you fall into the category of the people who have dreams but lack hope, I tell you today that your dreams can be accomplished; God is able to bring it to pass. God doesn't look at your background, your parent's status, or your qualification. Those things are irrelevant. All God cares about is that the desire He put in you comes to pass. Begin to fill your mind with the word of God and believe what He says concerning you. Each time your mind or other people call you stupid, tell yourself that Jesus said in Matthew 5:13 "I am the light of the world, I am the salt of this earth; I will succeed in all that I do."

Rekindle that desire you had as a child and believe that God can do beyond that. If you trust God enough, you will see Ephesians 3:20 come to pass in your life. Let God be your

164

greatest encourager. People will try to talk you out of it, but let God talk you in. God believes the best of you.

62255467R00106

Made in the USA
Charleston, SC
11 October 2016